CAROL BURMOOD & DESIREE SMITH-COLLIS

YOU ARE HERE

A GUIDE TO UNCOVERING YOUR
TRUE IDENTITY, PURSUING GREATNESS,
AND *building the life you love*

TWO PENNY
PUBLISHING

Copyright © 2021 Carol Burmood

Two Penny Publishing
850 E. Lime Street #266
Tarpon Springs, Florida 34688
TwoPennyPublishing.com
info@TwoPennyPublishing.com

All rights reserved. This book or parts thereof may not be reproduced in any form, stored in any retrieval system, or transmitted in any form by any means—electronic, mechanical, photocopy, recording, or otherwise—without prior written permission of the publisher, except as provided by United States of America copyright law.

Scripture quotations marked TPT are from The Passion Translation®. Copyright © 2017, 2018 by Passion & Fire Ministries, Inc. Used by permission. All rights reserved. ThePassionTranslation.com.

Scripture quotations marked NIV are taken from the Holy Bible, New International Version®, NIV®. Copyright © 1973, 1978, 1984, 2011 by Biblica, Inc.™ Used by permission of Zondervan. All rights reserved worldwide. www.zondervan.com. The "NIV" and "New International Version" are trademarks registered in the United States Patent and Trademark Office by Biblica, Inc.™

Scripture quotations marked NLT are from the Holy Bible, New Living Translation. © 1996, 2004, 2007, 2013, 2015 by Tyndale House Foundation. Used by permission of Tyndale House Publishers, Inc., Carol Stream, Illinois 60188. All rights reserved.

For permission requests and ordering information, email the publisher at:
info@twopennypublishing.com

Library of Congress Control Number: 2021915384

Paperback: 978-1-950995-48-6
eBook also available

FIRST EDITION

For information about this author, to book event appearance, or media interview, please contact the author representative at: info@twopennypublishing.com

table of contents

INTRO   **You Are Here**   5

PART ONE: **How Did I Get HERE?**
Chapter 1:   Rearview Mirror   17
Chapter 2:   You've Been Rerouted   37
Chapter 3:   Stuck Between a Rock and a Hard Place   63
Chapter 4:   The Making of a Mindset   87

PART TWO: **Building Your Dream**
Chapter 5:   You Were Created to Create   115
Chapter 6:   Why a Why   131
Chapter 7:   Stepping Into It   153
Chapter 8:   Confidence Matters   175

PART THREE: **Leveling Up ⬆ - Plan for Success**
Chapter 9:   Honing Your Habits   195
Chapter 10:   Own Your Morning   215
Chapter 11:   Forward Vision   233
Chapter 12:   Steadfast and Pursue   247

NOTES   259
ACKNOWLEDGMENTS   267
ABOUT THE AUTHORS   273

YOU ARE HERE

This book is about your dreams and purpose. It is about charting your course to pursue those aspirations you have held inside for so long. Whether the callings of those aspirations have grown dim or gotten louder over this last year, you know you need to DO something. We want you to know that having a vision and purpose for your life isn't only available to the select few. YOU have access to it too! It's available to me, and it's also available to you. ALL you have to do is be willing to believe it, chase it, develop it, form habits that attract it, and pour in the effort and work that will carry it to reality. Sounds easy enough, right?

We have all met face-to-face with a fork in the road, a moment of decision, pressing us to chart a course towards something more. We can choose to walk a path that will keep us content, safe in the parameters of what we already know, or we can choose to follow the faint whisper that there is a better path, one that leads to a life of purpose, fulfillment, happiness, and fullness beyond what we may have ever imagined for ourselves. This road will be different because it is unknown. The unknown can be terrifying because the cost of entry comes with confronting uncertainty and accepting failure. If you allow it, the great unknown can also be exhilarating because you've just awakened an excitement and energy that's been held deep inside you, waiting to be released. There will always be challenges and resistance along the way; fear of failure may intimidate you from taking new steps. But this time is different because you will be more prepared as you begin to walk in the direction of unlocking something inside you that you knew existed but could never find the formula to access it. Stepping into it takes courage, belief, and most of all, conviction. You were built for this! Once you experience the first step on the path of growth, you will begin to feel hopeful, energized, empowered, and equipped in your pursuit.

A true purpose is not about what you do, it's not about proving anything to the world. It's more about finding who you were made to be.

JORDAN LEE DOOLEY

We wrote this book from a place deep in our hearts that kept calling to us that there must be more for our lives. As that belief grew for us, it evolved into a message that we needed to share. A message for all to take notice of their own still voice saying… "there must be more." Our journey started by owning where we were in our lives and paying attention to what beliefs were driving our thoughts and decisions. In order to move towards a new path, we needed to honestly address our old habits and beliefs about ourselves to determine how we have been shaped by the world around us.

We used to believe...

➡️ We had to live within the perimeters that were defined by others.

➡️ What our negative inner voice said about us.

➡️ Amazing lives were reserved for other people.

➡️ We had to become "the expert" before getting started.

➡️ Our fear of failure is real and made perfect sense.

➡️ Our dreams were unrealistic according to our reality.

➡️ That getting up early in the morning was for early birds or hardcore people.

➡️ We were lazy and undisciplined.

➡️ Introverts can't be successful because they are not bold enough or assertive enough to take charge; that's just how I'm wired.

➡️ Our past would define our future, doomed forever to a mediocre life.

➡️ God doesn't have a plan for me or I missed it one too many times so He's moved on to someone else.

These are things that defined our life for far too long. Thoughts that limited our growth and potential of blossoming into the identity God intended for us. UNTIL... we started saying YES! After a series of Yes's in the same direction, new clarity came to us along with a dream to impact others. We wrote this book because we believe there is great power in sharing life experiences and successes.

We wanted to share the things that worked, the things that didn't work, and what made the most difference in our own growth. Our hope is to provide encouragement and streamline the process so others can join in on the path towards self-discovery and fulfillment.

Through trial and error, emotional storms, and learned-lessons, we have landed at the conclusion that life is meant to be lived and lived fully. We believe in depth and meaningful pursuits and want to encourage others to strive to find their place at the table. Somewhere along the road, our beliefs grew and changed to become more aligned with the image of God and the inherent purpose that exists in each one of us.

What we believe now

→ We are all made for more—EVERY ONE of us was created for impact!!

→ We have a choice in which voice we listen to.

→ An amazing life is available for us all.

→ Taking the first step is what leads to mastery.

→ Failure is a growth opportunity. You only fail if you don't get back up.

→ We were all given a dream to be pursued.

→ Morning routines are the driving force to smashing your goals.

➡ Awareness and intentions are game-changers.

➡ Introverts are powerful forces to be reckoned with.

➡ Finding your best life includes a solid WHY, healthy habits and assured confidence.

➡ There are God-opportunities everywhere. Don't miss them!

Reframing and reshaping our beliefs opened the door for new perspective and insight. It positioned us firmly on the path where we could begin building the life we love. Our goals are within our grasp. Even though we are not at our desired destination yet, we live full in each day, excited for what doors God will open next. We want to invite you on this journey with us!

You Are Here is Divided Into Three Parts

Here's how to read and get the most out of it.

Part 1: Is where you will come face to face with where you are and how you got there. Each chapter will help you step into a deeper working knowledge about how you got to where you are now. This process is essential to weeding out the untruths you've believed about yourself and moving past the blocks that have kept you from pursuing your God-given purpose in this life.

Part 2: Is where you will begin to walk towards your dream. Reaching, exploring, defining, and believing that it is not only possible but actually achievable. This is where your vision is expanded, and a new aliveness is experienced. During this phase, alignment, clarity, and passion come into focus, and momentum will start to build. It requires an open mind, open heart, and willingness to stretch beyond your comfort zone.

Part 3: Is where you will learn the tools that will give you new traction towards the WHY for your life. Success comes with a consistency of practicing them every day, taking those small steps to eventually reach those BIG goals and dreams you never thought were possible.

Each chapter is a piece or part of your life. These are not small things to conquer, they are threads in a tapestry of your life; when carefully and intentionally placed, they contribute to a beautiful and fulfilling life. These chapters offer knowledge to be gained and skills to develop through practice. Each idea is an important component to put into place on your journey. Which chapter speaks out to you in your present life? Use that chapter as a resource for your new beginning to move forward. Every section serves as a purposeful step into your new and improved future. There is a voice that has been calling to you over the years, and *now* is the time to listen to what it is saying. The chapters offer workable growth experiences that you can revisit as many times as needed to gain clarity. Allow each concept to breathe new life and inspiration into the journey ahead.

You get to dream, define, and develop your future.
Specific to you.
Deepen your practice and encounter joy daily.

When you begin working these concepts and practices together, the path begins to unfold.

You will discover deeper meaning, build stronger momentum, and create more movement towards achieving your dream.

It is in the commitment, diligent effort, and consistency where the fulfillment of God's plan for your life awakens and begins to take shape beyond what you could have ever imagined.

And so we thank you, Lord, for this is your book. The divine inception began because of you in our hearts. Your heart is for us to live in the fullness of ALL of the gifts and talents within us. It is when we strive to live to our fullest purpose and potential that we can impact the world as you intended. Like any parent, you desire this for your children. This written book is a pathway to get there. For some, this book will shine a bright light in a dimly lit tunnel of life. For others, the tunnel is behind them, but they aren't sure where or how to get to the places they want to be. And for everyone, we hope you will find the strength to pursue and fulfill your dreams and passions.

No matter where you are in life, there is something here for you. It doesn't matter what your past or present fears are, you can pursue your dreams… never give up! That is our message to you. It's not about what you have been through or had to figure out… it's about where you are going and the difference you can make in this world.

We believe in this so much because we have walked through each chapter of this book and applied it to our own lives. Through it all, we discovered new truths and harnessed the exploding power of our dreams for the future. Although all of our life stories are unique, the trajectory is the same. We all have a starting line, a beginning point, and as we travel through life we will without doubt come face-to-face with its many crossroads. The road before you holds wonderful opportunities to live out a full and satisfying life, and to bless those whom we cross paths with. The next chapter of your journey has not been written yet, it is up to you to decide where to go from here.

What's your story going to be?
Is it time to write a new chapter for your life?

We are here writing this book for you and for others who find themselves "somewhere" in life but not quite sure that "somewhere" is where they want to be. It was written for those who feel lost, trapped, and aimless. It was written for those who have a burning desire for more but lacking the skills to make it a reality.

You have everything you need to start today because YOU ARE HERE!!!

Where is **HERE?**
How did I get **HERE?**

HERE is a place where you
don't feel happy.

HERE is where you wonder
how it happened.

HERE is where you are not sure
what to do or how to change it.

One thing you know for sure,
is that you don't want to stay **HERE!**

PART 1

HOW DID I GET HERE?

REARVIEW MIRROR

To know where you are going you must first know where you've been and how you got HERE. All of us have a life map, a charted course from where we first began to where we are now. Through the years, we journey ahead, gaining information and encountering different experiences along the way. All of these events begin to shape how we view ourselves and how we view our potential next steps towards our goals and future.

We are products of the past, but
we don't have to be prisoners of it.

RICK WARREN

When we are at our best, we are moving forward and chasing greatness in our lives. We are filled with confidence, fueled by self-worth, and our passion and faith guide us towards our future. If we are not moving forward with positive energy, then some belief or experience from our past may be keeping us stuck where we are.

Today is the day to be OPEN to the idea that you were made for more. Let this be the moment you decide to change the course of where your life is going… forever!

Do you know anyone who appears to be living their best life and making their dreams come true? How many people do you see and you wish you were in their shoes? So, what is actually keeping you from reaching your dreams?

Perhaps you already have a clear vision and dream for the future, but your efforts keep falling short. Or maybe there are some barriers and roadblocks preventing you from breathing enough life or energy into your dream. You may no longer believe in your dream or believe in yourself like you once did. Your life may feel stagnant like you're not moving forward, stuck in place. Deep down, you know there has got to be more, that your dream is still out there somewhere. But, you are not sure what to do with your dreams or your feelings.

We are so glad you are here! You came to the right place. We are going to help you create your own personal "roadmap" to the life you were meant to live. It'll show you where to start, what roadblocks to look out for, and what tools to apply. This book will get you moving towards the places and feelings that you desire. You can do it!

Throughout the course of each chapter, we are going to take you on an experiential walk that will launch you into a new season of your life. An extraordinary season that you are destined to create and live out. It's easy to write these words, but it requires a lot more effort to do the work and make it happen.

Let's commit to transforming your current season into something brand new. You will never regret investing hard work, honesty, and hope into your future—this is the time to go all in. So, let's do it!

> And we know that God causes
> everything to work together for the good
> of those who love God and are called
> according to his purpose for them.
>
> ROMANS 8:28 (NLT)

We believe everyone can creatively develop a pathway to making their dreams come true. Everyone has purpose and passion inside of them, so that means every one of us can unleash and live them out. Most of us just need help learning how to do it. That's the heart and soul behind this book. There was a time when this book was a distant, hopeless idea. It changed course when we started to change our mindset and everyday behaviors. Our seed of possibility has grown into a full-fledged dream and reality! We want to share the steps and insights that brought this dream to fruition, so you too can discover and experience the purpose you were created for!

This will be a time for you to reflect, refine, and reset. Don't hold back from these challenges and opportunities. Be honest and authentic, but do not beat yourself up. Today is the day to be proud that you are doing the work to grow and feel joy for the hope of your future. Be willing to dream, try, and fail. Having a perfect past, present, or future is not a reality for anyone. BUT, learning from the past, preparing in the present, and hoping for the future IS!

This process will be a life-changing journey of learning to value yourself, finding your purpose, and creating a life you love. As you read this, you will either say, "WOW, that's awesome! Let's do it!" or "Gee, I don't know if that is possible for me." If you are the latter and don't believe you deserve a life of greatness, this book is especially for you! We hope to fill you with the right dose of encouragement, inspiration, and motivation to open your mind.

You are HERE. You are exactly where you are supposed to be, but not where you are meant to stay. You have reached the first step towards changing your life when you realize you don't want to stay HERE anymore!

Put on your comfortable shoes. YOU SAID YES!

You said yes, and that means you are at least curious enough to turn the page to the next chapter to see if just MAYBE there is a way for you to follow that inner voice. That voice speaking hope, courage and keeps saying, "Yes, there is more than this." There is more growth, more joy, more love, more resources, and more impact than you could ever imagine. Maybe you haven't heard that inner voice in a long time. The world around us is often loud and full of noise, drowning out our inner voice and confidence. But, even in the chaos of life, our inner voice still wonders and whispers about the future.

➡ "Is this all there is to my life?"

➡ "There's so much more that I wanted to do."

➡ "What is my purpose? Why am I here?"

➡️ "I'm so stuck and unhappy at my job. It's not fulfilling."

➡️ "I know there is something great I am supposed to do."

Saying YES gives your inner voice permission to dream beyond wonder, and boldly proclaim your purpose and passion. This is just the beginning of what will undoubtedly be a long, exciting journey. But before you begin on this voyage of discovery, it is vital that you gain an overview of how you got here so you don't repeat it. Sometimes, to pursue what is in front of us, we must first release the way we see ourselves and the behaviors that no longer serve us. So let's get started!

HOW DO YOU VIEW "YOU?"

Your view of "You" goes everywhere you go. Have you ever thought about that?

Your view of "You" includes your:

➡️ Childhood history

➡️ Cultural and faith-based values

➡️ Confidence level

➡️ Self-worth/Value

➡️ Limiting beliefs & fears

➡️ Self-doubt

We are shaped by a lot of things, and sometimes we give too much power and too much influence to the wrong things. Instead of holding tight to our purpose and passion, we may build our self-worth out of broken images from our past. Misaligned from our true self, we often miss the enjoyment and adventure that each day offers.

The life that lies before you is like a beautiful ocean packed with endless possibilities and invigorating wonders. Struggling with self-image, a faulty view of "You" is like sitting alone on the shore and watching the wavers but never experiencing the power. Someone or something has influenced you to believe that you cannot swim, you cannot float, and you are the person who watches and not the person who dives in.

This is the person who went on your last job interview, your last date, a family event, and who showed up to your last work meeting. This is the person who shows up in your marriage, guides your children, and navigates the decisions of your days. A person who feels held back, withdrawn, and unsure of how or when to finally take a refreshing dip into the water.

Answer this question honestly: Have you been bringing the best version of yourself along with you through your recent days and events?

Yes _____ No _____ Need to think about it _____

Identifying and owning how you currently view yourself is paramount to moving forward. No one can make a change without first acknowledging that there is room to grow. Even if we have a track record of growth and have experienced seasons of joy, there is still more! Don't give up on tomorrow! The moment you can acknowledge that you have more life to explore and enjoy is the moment you can begin to leave the outdated self-image in the dust and define a future view of yourself that will take you where you want to go. But first, let's keep our focus in the rearview mirror to better understand how the past has shaped your perspective about life.

While growing up, how often did you hear words of encouragement? Or, perhaps a better question is, how often did you feel discouraged or hear negativity?

You may have received a lot of discouragement and negativity as you dreamed, tried, and perhaps even failed. Over time, deep down inside you started to believe those negative thoughts were true. Eventually, your innate curiosity was stifled and now you avoid trying to learn new things. This type of programming changed the way you viewed yourself and the world. Suddenly you start to live smaller, feel stuck, and unknowingly begin to settle for less. These moments have a massive impact on us. Over the years, those beliefs and views influenced our present-day thought patterns and behaviors. Oftentimes, they become so automatic that we don't question why we are behaving a certain way.

There will always be external circumstances outside your control: financial insecurity, substance abuse, mental health issues, medical and personal loss, and trauma. All of these skew our outlook on our future and the possibilities that it holds. Hope for a future never really stood a chance when it feels as if the universe is plotting against us. Perhaps you have actually felt that way and said it out loud, that you "just aren't cut out for something" or that "things just don't go my way." Those thoughts are like weeds growing in our heart and mind, and it takes a lot of work to find and pull the roots out. But when we do, it makes room for something beautiful to grow.

> Jesus looked at them intently and said,
> 'Humanly speaking, it is impossible.
> But with God everything is possible.'
>
> MATTHEW 19:26 (NLT)

Life from Your Perspective

Let's assess how you view life from your present perspective. Each of us has a lens through which we filter our thoughts, ideas, and dreams. It is a POINT OF ACCESS that our life flows through. It is where we decide how we want to live out our everyday aspirations.

Is your perspective negative, limited, fixed, defeating, or skeptical?

Or is your perspective more open to growth, change, hopeful, and willing to try?

To help identify life from your perspective, we are offering two camps from which you view the world. We typically either operate from a FIXED mindset or a GROWTH mindset. We included some potential thoughts, attitudes, and postures under each so that you can determine which most represents your current state of mind. Circle the phrase you identity with on the chart below.

FIXED Mindset VS·	GROWTH Mindset
I can't do that.	It can happen.
I'm too old.	I have so much time left.
Pessimistic attitude.	Optimistic nature.
I should be better than I am.	I believe in myself.
I'm a failure.	I'm open to grow.
What if something bad happens?	Failing is a part of growing.
It won't happen for me.	I'm passionate about this.

While examining these two mindsets, which best represents your perspective on life in your past and present?

There are a multitude of scenarios throughout the course of each day where we have the opportunity to act from either a growth mindset or a fixed mindset. We can even use both mindsets inside of the same day! Knowing that two mindsets exist will help us consciously decide which one to choose. You can access the power of choice and make a REAL-TIME decision about which lens you want to use. If you haven't already done so, now is the time to embrace a growth mindset. Your future life depends on it!

A New Day, A New Story

How you wake up in the morning is a determining factor of how your day will go. A negative mood in your morning will most likely carry throughout your day. Any type of pessimism or anxiety about your life will likely keep you locked into a fixed mindset. If you have a pessimistic view of life, you may not be a person that sets any goals for yourself because you already determined it doesn't matter if you do. If, by chance, you do happen to muster up enough effort to try, you are more likely to get frustrated quickly and give up. Consequently, an anxious mind spinning with fear and insecurity will drive your moods and decisions, thus closing you off to new growth and new opportunities.

On the other hand, research shows that people who consider themselves "optimists" often manage to overcome obstacles with more success than pessimists. This is because the stories they tell themselves motivate them to work harder when the going gets tough. If you are facing any type of life challenge and the story you tell yourself is "I can't possibly do this," guess what… you won't even make it to the starting line. If you reframe that narrative with "What can I learn from this experience?" you will have created the self-talk necessary to position yourself at the starting line. At the very least, you'll have a shot at running the race.

> We tell ourselves stories
> in order to live.
>
> JOAN DIDION

What story are you telling yourself? As you can see, different stories lead to different outcomes. Are you promoting a version that will keep you feeling stuck in the life you have been living up until this point? You may believe you don't have the skill set or talent to achieve anything greater; therefore, it must be beyond your capability, so why even try? Too many of us avoid pursuing anything outside our comfort zone because somewhere we bought into the belief that we can't grow or develop through practice. So we dodge anything that challenges us and instead opt for the easy road because it's familiar and safe.

Let's pause and take a look at two very different versions of how we frame the stories we tell ourselves. Pay close attention to the one that will validate your old story versus the one that opens the door to new growth and opportunity—notice which mindset story paves the way for your spirit to flourish.

One day, out of nowhere, your friend comes shooting at you like a rocket, with uncontained enthusiasm asking you if you want to partner up and write a book. Before you have a chance to sidestep out of the way, you get so caught up in the excitement you accidentally say YES. Suddenly, you are flooded with fear as you take a giant gulp of "What did I just do?" You can't possibly write a book; you've never even taken a creative writing class. Seriously, you can hardly speak in full sentences, so how can you be expected to string enough words together to fill the pages of an entire chapter? Plus, you're way too old to take on this kind of assignment. What if you can't live up to the expectations of other people? What if you can't live up to the expectations of yourself? And by the way, why would anyone care about what you have to say anyway?

OR, one day, here comes your friend, shooting at you like a rocket, with the type of enthusiasm one would have after winning the lottery to ask you if you want to partner up and write a book. This has silently been on your heart for years, and you can't believe this opportunity just presented itself. Before you have a chance to say, "I'm all in," you get caught up in the excitement and start brainstorming all the things you may want to write about. You take a giant gulp of faith as you begin to think of all the growth and learning you'll get to do. You are flooded with pure joy because you've always wanted to write a book, and even though you've never taken a creative writing class, you can't wait to learn something new. Seriously, you can hardly wait to expand your vocabulary, so you begin speaking in complete sentences to all your friends. And by complete, I mean run-on, so you can practice using all your newly discovered words. You are open to this challenge and passionate about stringing enough words together to fill the pages of an entire chapter. You have a lot of living under your belt and have so much life experience to offer the world. The only way you can fail is if you decide not to write the book. By the way, there are so many people who need to hear what you have to say.

As you can see, your mindset and view of self carries the power to impact the course of your life greatly. People with a growth mindset believe they can achieve their goals and dreams, even when they aren't entirely sure how to do it. They are more open to learning ways to grow both personally and professionally so they can fuel their passion and purpose. This is what sets them apart from those who work from a fixed mindset.

You see things, and you say 'why?'
But I dream of things that never
were, and I say 'Why not?'

GEORGE BERNARD SHAW

Raise your hand if you want to work from a place of "Why Not?" and allow yourself the space to grow into the adventure that awaits you?

Count me in (thumbs up) _____

Now you have a better understanding of how your story influences everyday decision making. When we make decisions, we are evaluating through a filter with many assumptions, judgments, possible lies, and worries about ourselves and our life story. For most of us, any decision requiring confidence or optimism will be undermined by the negative limitations of our filter.

Did you know we make approximately 35,000 decisions in a day?
Have you ever caught yourself saying, "What was I thinking?"

Research indicates that most of the decisions we make, even when we think we are logical, are made unconsciously and involve our emotions. This is surprising and can be a bit scary when we add the emotional aspect to it. Sometimes we will make a decision based on emotion without realizing it. Feeling excited, anxious, sad, angry, and even embarrassed can lead us into a series of decisions that may not be best for us. We make our best decisions when we take our emotions into account and find the balance between understanding and wisdom.

Your life is the sum result of all the choices you make, both consciously and unconsciously. If you can control the process of choosing, you can take control of all aspects of your life. You can find the freedom that comes from being in charge of yourself.

ROBERT BENNETT

It's time to take back the power you have been freely giving away. We are here to get honest and talk about the real stuff—the stuff hiding in the dark corners of your life—because we don't want you to miss out on all that's available to you. As you begin to peel back the layers, a new awareness will emerge. Don't be surprised to face things you may have been avoiding or didn't realize existed. We want you to open yourself up to the beauty of the journey and rediscover the joy of dreaming once again.

No matter how much life we have in the rearview mirror, we have all been given the gift of the present and the hope of the future. Whether you are a fresh-faced 20-something, or a little further along with some wear and tear on your spirit, your dreams <u>do not expire</u>. Every decision you have made so far has led you to this exact spot, for this exact moment, for a purpose specific to you. God's plans are always good, and His timing is always perfect. You are exactly where you are supposed to be. You are HERE.

You are **HERE**
where past hurts will no longer dictate
the terms of your future.

You are **HERE**
where there is a stirring in your soul.

You are **HERE**
where you are beginning to
wonder what's ahead.

You are **HERE**
where a new story is
beginning to take shape.

YOU'VE BEEN REROUTED

Remember those old-style GPS devices that suctioned to your windshield? Even though they blocked half your peripheral vision, you were so excited to have one because you'd never have to buy a map again. The GPS had one purpose, to guide you to your destination and get you to the place that you wanted to go.

Imagine planning and preparing an amazing trip and inputting the address of your dream destination into your GPS or phone. Can you picture it now, the place that your heart and soul are calling out for? This is the place you have always wanted to go, this is the place that you've prayed about and imagined for so long. You have a dream, you have a destination, what could possibly go wrong?

Well… actually, a couple of things can go wrong.

Perhaps all you see is the spinning, rerouting icon because the destination has not yet been uploaded into the cloud, where somehow every coordinate in the universe is stored. You have been driving in the same circle being rerouted by a machine that doesn't even know how to enunciate syllables properly.

Or your focus is in the wrong place, and you may have missed your turn and now you've ended up off of the path to where you intended to go. Maybe the navigating system paused for a moment, and then it informs you that the path has now changed. You have been rerouted. Your destination hasn't changed, but you have, and so your next steps are going to be a little different. Failure to follow directions or make the correct turn doesn't ruin your chances of getting to your destination; it simply adds time to your travel and causes you to pay extra close attention as you get back on track.

There are a multitude of other issues that can arise at any time. You may find yourself losing connection to the navigation system, which can be a very frustrating experience. You have a source for information and direction, but the signal may weaken or get blocked, leaving you with this spinning wheel or loading screen. Something is limiting your ability to move forward with confidence, so now you must either wait for the signal to return or try your best to move forward without any plan. The interference has not removed your end goal or destination; it is simply limiting your belief in how to get where you dreamed of going. The spinning wheel on your GPS screen might as well be spinning tires stuck in the mud. "Rerouting" is what you hear as you try to reconnect to the route and move on from HERE.

This is what happens when limiting beliefs, low self-worth, shame, and anxiety enter into our subconscious.

You see, we were all designed with the expectation to live an extraordinary life of purpose—a life where there are no limits, no boundaries, no blocking of the signal whose sole purpose is to guide you down your desired path. We were all made for greatness, but somewhere along the road, our signal got blocked, and we were rerouted. We were rerouted to a life with limitations that restrict our decisions and secure us to boundaries that force us to spin in a confined space. It supplies us with just enough interference to drown out the voice calling us to pursue a life of richness. Even if the voice calling out to us miraculously makes its way through the static in a moment of clarity, we still can't seem to make sense of the coordinates. Rather than reaching the sweet spot you were destined for, you are stuck spinning in the same circle.

However, your destination and dreams have not moved; they are still there waiting for you to get back on the path that will ultimately lead you to them. Something is either taking your attention away from your next steps, or limiting and weakening your connection to them. You need to understand what is behind the spinning circles.

Roadblocks & Wrong Turns

So, what causes us to stumble on our journey? One of the larger culprits that we need to address our limiting beliefs. Limiting beliefs are super powerful and highly influential in our macro and micro-decisions, actions, and thoughts. This belief system can take root in our heart and mind and push its way to the center of our worldview, wreaking havoc on our self-esteem. It is like a virus that hacks into our navigation system, dropping roadblocks in front of us and whispering wrong directions in our ears. Let's take a look at the range of impacts that limiting beliefs can have and how they carry the potential to hold you back from what you're capable of achieving.

A Limiting Belief

➡️ Defines for you what is good or bad, real or impossible.

➡️ Utilizes emotional reliance while overlooking the facts.

➡ Undermines the action steps you take.

➡ Bridles your passion, cuts off your energy.

➡ Affects every relationship; personal, work, spiritual.

➡ Directly affects your health and happiness.

➡ Creates an adaptive version of your true self.

To put it simply: limiting beliefs LIMIT YOU!

This is why it is important to be wise to what you truly believe about yourself. Seek real truth, not the empty negativity.

> Your beliefs organize
> the world for you.
>
> STEVE SISGOLD

According to some really smart people on Google, a **limiting belief** is your mind's way of protecting you from a dangerous or difficult situation when you were younger. More precisely, when you experienced an EMOTIONALLY overwhelming situation in your past, your mind looked for a way to help protect you. Since we were not yet equipped to think logically about those situations, the brain helps by programming us how to behave differently so we don't put ourselves in harm's way again. When our mind senses any potential threat, our thought processes and behaviors begin to integrate at a very deep and subconscious level. The program repeats so often that the behavior becomes an automatic process and occurs without us making a conscious decision. At an earlier time in our lives, this served a purpose—to protect us from doing something that may cause us harm. However, as we evolve and accumulate new information, we become more and more qualified to make different decisions about those beliefs.

The challenge with limiting beliefs is that we are constantly in battle with the real truth and the truth we have designed to protect ourselves emotionally. Even though this self-created truth once kept us safe, it now serves a self-sabotaging purpose. Regardless if it holds any remnants of truth or not, it has become your truth, but it is not "the" truth. How often have you told yourself the same version, so many times, that you now believe it? If you challenged it in the slightest way, it would fall flat on its face. But we do not usually challenge what we already believe to be true.

A limiting belief may have been formed to protect you from that past pain, and your system is placing roadblocks ahead of you so you are less inclined to travel down that road again. The problem is, it can linger far too long in your system. Something that was once true, "I should not ____ because ____," may not be true anymore.

So, a limiting belief wants to **reroute** us from anything that may slightly resemble a previous experience that has caused hurt or pain. The course of our life continuously gets rerouted to follow the same, familiar, worn pathways of thoughts and behaviors. We are led to travel in a safe little circle without going anywhere new. Can you think of a limiting belief from your past that may have been true for that time or season? More importantly, can you recognize a limiting belief in your system that has far overstayed its welcome? Have you been avoiding something because of the pain or discomfort that may come from trying something new or growing out of your old routes and dusty roads?

It's not what you say out of your mouth that determines your life, it's what you whisper to yourself that has the most power.

ROBERT T. KIYOSAKI

Let's explore this some more. We all have limiting beliefs in our past, and so we must all be vigilant in clearing them from the path before us.

As a child, were you told by someone close to you that you wouldn't be able to do something? Sometimes they are subtle suggestions or passing statements that make their way deep into our souls. Perhaps you always wanted to be a competitive swimmer, but your parents mentioned in a moment of what they thought was "sparing you from disappointment" that it was okay to get second place. You took that seemingly simple thought and carried the theme forward. This happened for me over time; I began to associate second place with being a loser, and thus the limiting belief was activated. There came a point when growing up I started to believe I was a "loser" and could never win the first-place medal on the swim team; henceforth, I learned to be okay with second place. My limiting belief that it was okay to be second meant I wasn't really cut out for first-place in anything. And even though I did have a spot on sports teams and got decent grades, my view of self became skewed in a diminishing kind of way that traveled with me for many years. That self-limiting belief did just that; it limited me, which was counter to who I was created to be and what I was created to accomplish.

This generated a huge internal conflict for me. I fully accepted the lie and belief that I would never be first. My coping response to this agreement was to adopt an "I don't care" attitude. This attitude followed me into my early twenties, rerouting me as I searched for happiness in all the wrong places and led me downhill into a not-so-proud-of-myself season. I now know this was my unconscious way to cope with the disappointment of not fulfilling my dreams of doing something great in this world.

Despite all my self-sabotaging decisions, somehow, by the grace of God, there was this small part of me that kept fighting for something better and I managed to graduate from college. But even that accomplishment wasn't enough to kill the noise of my second-place thinking. Once again, I was rerouted on the path of life. Things continually got worse, relationships fell apart, and so did my view of myself. My vision for life had become very small and dark, and I lost sight of who I was created to be for several years. I followed the trail of reinforcing all the negative themes that became behaviors until I landed myself at the bottom. This is how it can happen to anyone; a story of persistent limiting beliefs rerouting the direction of our lives.

Which is why we cannot emphasize this enough... walking towards greatness all starts with changing how you see yourself. One day the Lord reached down into my mess and opened a door for me to say YES to being in first place. From that day forward, my life has never been the same. With a tiny mustard seed of faith in my heart, I was able to start climbing my way out of the second place hole I had been living in for far too long; and I have never looked back!

As new, healthy beliefs grew, the old limiting beliefs lost their power and faded away. These new beliefs birthed a new vision for my life's purpose. A vision that allowed me to see a new destination aligned with God's bigger plan for me.

What is <u>your</u> limiting belief?

It is a constant theme that runs through your life and affects your mindset without you knowing it. Perhaps your father left when you were young, so you felt rejected and believed that you were unworthy of love. As a result, you have a difficult time trusting others. You don't put yourself out there or open up to trusting as a means to protect yourself from being hurt, effectively placing limits on you. So, when that new job opportunity comes up and you meet all the requirements and qualifications, you shrink into the background because you don't believe it can happen for you. You don't buy into the notion that you are capable and worthy of greater things like advancing in your career, because this story fits more in line with all the others you've told yourself.

There is an inner voice to our limiting belief that speaks to us when faced with situations that question our worth and value. You might hear:

➡️ I can't do X because of Y.

➡️ I'm not good enough.

➡️ I'm not smart enough.

➡️ I'm not worthy enough.

➡️ I'm afraid I will fail or make a big mistake.

➡️ I'm selfish for wanting more.

➡️ I'm not educated or smart enough.

➡️ I'm not performing to my expectations.

➡️ _____

So, let's do a little exercise here in real-time, like right now. Set your timer!

Take a quick inventory to see if you can identify your limiting beliefs. If it doesn't come to you right away, don't worry, you can revisit this later.

On a personal level, what do you feel is holding you back?

_____

What are some things you are afraid of?

_____

Based on your current view of yourself, what limiting belief(s) becomes obvious to you?

_____

How do you feel the decisions based on your limiting beliefs affected the progress of your life?

_____

Is there a constant theme in your life that you can identify at this time?

_____

How has it affected your SELF-WORTH? Do you feel better or worse about yourself?

_____

Remember, the function of limiting beliefs was necessary and somewhat helpful when we were younger. However, as we mature we are not even aware of the beliefs we filter our daily life experiences through and carry around like dead weight. Every limiting belief comes with a cost. Measuring the cost of your limits will help you better understand how problematic they have become. Once you identify yours, you will want to begin calculating the price you are unknowingly paying. It is almost like using a credit card, the process of spending one dollar is the same as one thousand—only the receipt shows a difference in cost. When you stop following your dreams and shelter in place, it can take a heavy toll on your heart, mind, and soul. Deep down, you know you are missing something.

What are some things you're **not** doing because of your limiting belief? How has it impacted and changed the trajectory of your life? Are they keeping you behind the scenes, content with playing small? Are you staying in the comfort of what's familiar to you? Do you want to sacrifice another year, until you find yourself ten years deep into not pursuing your calling or dream because you're too scared to challenge your beliefs?

You see, a limiting belief holds power to demonstrate defiance against new opportunities that have always been available to you. The result is, we grow up not living to our full potential, not taking any risks, and not looking beyond the door of pursuing our dreams. We end up with a mediocre, unfulfilled, average, "It's-safe-so-who-are-we-to-ask-for-more?" kind of life. Is second place living going to be okay with you?

The good news is, you have a choice; you can either repeat or evolve.

Tomorrow is a new day. If the today version of you doesn't change one thing, you are destined to repeat the same tomorrow. We will give you the tools that will help you grow later down the road.

> You begin to fly when you let go
> of self-limiting beliefs and allow
> your mind and aspirations to rise to
> greater heights.
>
> BRIAN TRACY

FEAR of Past Failures, other people's judgment, unknowns, uncertainty

Let's take a moment right now to pull FEAR out of the dark corner it hides in and expose it for what it really is. Why? Because this thief is robbing you of an abundant life—a life full of new and exciting experiences, a life of wonder, a life beyond what any fear-induced life could ever imagine. It's important to understand that we are not talking about the healthy fear that gives us a brief pause, slows us down from impulsive behavior, or recognizes when there's danger ahead. What we are talking about here is the kind of fear that shows up dressed incognito to crash your party. You didn't recognize it, and nobody around you knew who it was. It may have even acted as a friend of a friend, so you let it in. Fear says it wants to protect you; the truth is, it wants to keep you from getting to your intended place in this world.

Fear is you imagining the worst.
Faith is you imagining
a higher purpose.

TONY ROBBINS

For some of us, fear will present itself as a slight hesitation. Healthy, right? Some of us could use a little more hesitation in our lives—especially all of you who can envision yourself skipping through the mall on a spending spree without even glancing at your bank account first. However, most of us allow this hesitation to talk us right out of the adventure and desires of our hearts. Inspiration appears, and fear tries to quickly blow it away. We chalk it up as just another passing thought, a crazy idea during a brief moment of insanity. We might even be thankful for not having to follow through with our big, audacious idea. Whew, thank you, Lord, I didn't act on it… Oh wait, that wasn't you?

For too long, I allowed fear to dictate the direction of my life. I grew up with a survival mentality. I did not leave much room for mistakes, always erring on the side of caution. There was no safety net to catch me if I fell, and the knowledge of this meant I was required to walk forward in life, carefully avoiding anything that slightly resembled risk. Don't take any chances and you won't have to worry about smashing face-first into the hard-concrete bottom. At least, this is what FEAR told me. I did life nowhere near the edge. I walked right in the middle of the safest part of the path with bumpers on both sides, just in case a glimpse of purpose or adventure could make its way through.

Then one day, I somehow collected enough courage to conquer this fear—or maybe it took the day off, or passed out at the party it wasn't invited to—and I did something brave. I bought a house when I was a single mom of two at the immature young age of twenty-three. Looking back, I remember how terrified I was. I mean, I can't predict the future! Anything could go wrong at any minute! A downward spiral of fear was now in full force. What if I lose my job? What if there are major repairs I can't afford? What if a hurricane pummels my home? What if one of my kids gets sick? Believe me; this decision did not go down without a risk assessment evaluation. After careful consideration of every possible outcome and what-ifs, I miraculously pushed forward through the uncertainty. And guess what? This was one of the best decisions I ever made!

Think of a time when you were able to quiet the fear, even though you were terrified or had a swarm of what-if concerns. Identify a moment you pushed forward just far enough to experience the freedom that comes from unlocked shackles falling to the floor. How did you feel? Empowered? Limitless? Unconstrained? Now hold on to that feeling, put it in your pocket, don't lose it, and guard it like your life depends on it. You are going to need it later.

For many of us, FEAR comes in all shapes and sizes. It has the ability to slide under the radar undetected for years and years. It provides the perfect conditions for stagnation, inaction, and possible paralysis of the heart. For others, it has a more profound impact on our livelihoods. It wreaks havoc; and, if not checked, will display itself as debilitating anxiety. This can happen so often it begins to convince you this is your normal state of mind. "This is how God wired you and there is nothing you can do about it. God made you to be overly critical and cautious so you may as well start accepting it." Please know this is a lie. We were not made to live in self-constructed prisons that confine us and keep us from intentionally moving with passion and purpose.

Fear has a way of disguising itself as practical, sensible, logical. By not calling out fear and recognizing it for what it is, we give it the power to keep us from pursuing our dreams and goals. Growing like a weed, it distorts our vision, hindering us from seeing opportunities as what they are, precious gifts from God.

Every time we choose safety,
we reinforce fear.

CHERI HUBER

Let's take a look at some of the different ways fear shapes our future life:

Past Failures: What do your past failures have to say about you, anyway? A LOT! They speak to the places where we already feel most vulnerable and weak. If you let them, your past failures will subtly take control over how you live in the present and in the future. Pay attention if you have a tendency to lean towards the safe bet. Are you afraid to step outside of your comfort zone? Do you pass on opportunities because your past failures are constantly there to remind you how you missed the mark previously?

Other People's Judgment: Other people's opinions matter to us greatly, especially when it comes from someone in our inner circle. By default, we automatically believe that the people closest to us know us as well as we know ourselves, and vice versa. We may assume to know how they will react to our passionate idea or step of faith, but we don't. And we also cannot equate their opinion with the inspiration of our heart or the call of God in our lives. You may have a close friend who frequently places their own limiting beliefs and fears on you. If that is the case, maybe it's time to reassess who you let in your inner circle? Words are powerful and carry the potential to build us up or tear us down. Carefully choose who you are allowing to speak into your life and how much weight you give their words.

Uncertainty: How many of us journey through this life with complete certainty in every decision we make? The kind of certainty that is free of doubt and full of assurance? Uh, nobody. Uncertainty is an active part of life. If we knew exactly what we were doing every moment of every day, what fun would be left to discover? Yet, this same feeling of uncertainty prevents us from fully diving into the life and opportunity that surrounds us.

As we turn the bend and begin working on casting out all fear,

let's take an honest look at some of the other limitations we may
have accepted.

Shame Changes Us!

Shame is the feeling that "there is something wrong with me,"
and we may feel stupid or worthless. When this occurs, our brain
overreacts as if we are facing physical danger, setting off our "fight-
or-flight" responses. Often this causes us to will do things in an
attempt to become invisible.

My ten-speed bike was my most prized possession. Mostly
because I knew my parents couldn't afford it but also because it was
the fastest way for me to transport my carefree spirit. It was a soft
yellow color, and just the right size for my tomboyish frame. I rode
that bike everywhere. "Hair blowing, hands in the air like you just
don't care," kind of everywhere. At this age, I didn't really give much
consideration to what other people thought of me. I understand
many of us say this out loud to ourselves in an effort to protect our
egos, all the while caring deeply about what other people think of us.
I can assure you; this was not the case here. At the innocent, naive,
"oblivious to the planet existing around me" age, I truly didn't know
I was supposed to care.

I rode this bike all around town proudly wearing my bright yellow
Hulk Hogan t-shirt. My chin high, smile wide, and completely free
from any shame whispering in my ear, "Girls who watch wrestling
are weird and strange." I was nine, and any feelings of shame had

not yet settled their way into my malleable awareness. I was still free to be who I was, free to express myself, free to explore the wide-open world in whatever t-shirt my little heart desired.

I grew up watching wrestling. It embodied every aspect of my life. My dad would order every pay-per-view event, and I mean every single one. He'd let me stay up late, even on a school night, so I didn't miss out on one second of the action. We were lucky enough to own a VHS recorder, so I would record them and relish in the drama one, or more accurately, several more times. I even seriously, or at least seriously as a nine-year-old can dream, envisioned myself being the first female wrestler. If you know me today, I understand how that's going to be a difficult image to reconcile because there were no women wrestlers back in the '80s. Oh, you thought it was because I was 5'2 and could barely jump 6 inches off the ground, let alone land a dropkick. No silly, women wrestlers were unheard of at the time, but I was up for challenging that notion.

Fast forward to today, where this is not a story I share often. Or actually, EVER. Never would I share this with another human being, not even my own children. I don't tell people I grew up so infatuated with Hulk Hogan that I once waited four hours in line for a ten-second encounter to get his autograph and nearly passed out from all the excitement. Then there was the jacket. I'm talking about a windbreaker jacket with a full-sized picture of Hulk Hogan's face which appeared to be painted by some world-class artist. I worked so hard to raise the sixty dollars it cost to own this one-of-a-kind masterpiece that could only be ordered through a catalog, so you knew it was special. This meant weeks of built-up anticipation. When it finally arrived, I wore that jacket everywhere. I didn't care that it was summertime in Florida or that I was the only kid in school who was lucky enough to own one. I truly never gave one iota to what people thought. It never occurred to me that I should be embarrassed or ashamed. I was who I was at that moment, and I loved every piece of myself.

So what happened? Why did I stop sharing this story, this part of myself I once shared so proudly? Why do I turn ten shades of red if my family members mention it to a group of strangers? Who invited shame into my narrative? When did a piece of who I was become so cringe-worthy I'd rather climb into a deep dark hole and hide than face the laughter and embarrassment of this secret getting revealed? Somewhere along the road, we apply a negative narrative to our stories and give shame permission to come along for the ride. Little do we know how deeply this subtle thief will take residence in our souls.

Shame is a powerful emotion whose mission is to rob, steal, and destroy. Its filter carries the capacity to change the trajectory of our life and shrink our existence. When we operate our lives from a place of shame, we become so caught up in trying to contain this negative emotion that we reduce ourselves to living in isolation. As a result, any freedom we would otherwise have access to is limited, greatly affecting how we express ourselves to the world.

When we play our lives backward, we can often pinpoint where shame enters and begins setting up camp - because it plans to stay for a while. I don't know the exact moment, but I do know it happened somewhere in my late teens. Sometime after, I was made fun of and mocked so many times that I took the jacket off and hid it in the far back corner of my closet, never to be showcased again. This is the price of shame. We begin to stuff pieces of ourselves away, hiding them until, if we are lucky enough, even we can forget they ever existed. For the unlucky, shame resurfaces, and we continually put time and energy into blending into the background in order to keep us out of the line of someone else's judgment. Is there something you've hidden away? Maybe a piece of yourself that you once loved because of an external experience? Did this cause you to begin applying a negative perspective to your internal belief about yourself? Until you release yourself from the suffocating grip of shame, your identity will become captive to the lies. You will be bound to walk through life constrained and reluctant to open any doors that present themselves.

Shame derives its power from being unspeakable… If we speak shame, it begins to wither. Just the way exposure to light was deadly for the gremlins, language and story bring light to shame and destroy it.

BRENÉ BROWN

There is good news.

Shame will tremble at the sound of truth.

Self-Worth

There is a direct correlation for people who carry shame to have a propensity for low self-worth.

How would you assess your self-worth and value today?

What is it based on?

What's blocking your view to a positive you?

Shame works in opposition to self-worth. The more you allow shame to take root, the more it covers over and chips away at your self-worth. If you carry shame in your life, it will never allow your self-worth to rise above it.

It turns out that there is a way for us to call shame out and reframe its meaning to a more healthy perspective. By doing so, its influence over our self-worth loses all authority. We can begin to see ourselves in a different light—the kind of natural lighting where imperfections, blemishes, and deficiencies fade into the distance and are overshadowed by value, acceptance, and belief in our gifts and talents. This is where pure hope for our future emerges.

This is key because self-worth is particularly important to our pursuit of goals and moving forward through life. Have you ever noticed when you are feeling really good about yourself, you are more OPEN to doing things you might not have considered before?

There you are, putting on your most eye-catching outfit, coiffuring your hair, perhaps some red lipstick gets put to good use. You're feeling super strong and confident! Whereas, if you are feeling down on yourself, you are more likely to be CLOSED off to taking chances or moving towards your dreams. These could be the days spent with an old T-shirt, with unwashed hair, eating day-old pizza. Can you relate to those times in your life? If the old T-shirt is more of your norm, be assured this process of finding the best version of yourself is going to have you dressing up more often and pursuing the life you have always wanted!

[Your self-worth] isn't based on the things you have accomplished or what others think of you—it comes from within. It is a deep knowing that you have value, that you are loveable, necessary to this life, and of incomprehensible worth.

DR. CHRISTINA HIBBERT

When God created you and placed you in this world, He placed inside you some greatness to be lived out, only by you. He gave us a life worthy of being lived, loved, and experienced as we stay true to who He calls us to be. You are still that person of great worth, no matter what has happened to you, no matter what your situation is or what people have told you. Here's the good news; your worth and value are redeemable! Your worth is a shimmering treasure deep down inside your soul. It's been covered over by the twists and turns in your journey, and now you get to search for it. You were created to love yourself so you can love others. Without the light of your worth, it will be difficult to shine out to others and the world.

You got rerouted.

As a counselor, I have heard endless stories about how people have gone from bright and courageous to living so down on themselves; they don't believe they deserve good things for their life. Having low self-esteem affects every relationship and decision you make, and you will pursue and achieve less in your life. This is such a tragic place to find yourself.

You hold within you everything needed for change. It's there patiently waiting for you to unlock it. But to access it, you must first let go of the weight, heaviness, and fear that is holding you hostage to your current circumstance. Once you shine the light and call it to the surface, you can begin speaking the truth and make a course correction to your destiny. Hopefully, you have been able to gain some insights and learn more about yourself and how you got to this point in your life. We know this can feel hard and painful—but it is necessary to unlocking an abundant future. It takes courage, but we believe that you may have a sense there really could be more for you, a better YOU ahead.

You are **HERE**
uprooting the lies you've been told.

You are **HERE**
believing you are worthy.

You are **HERE**
opening up to more.

You are **HERE**
preparing for change.

STUCK BETWEEN A ROCK AND A HARD PLACE

No one likes to be stuck. And yet, we can too often find ourselves standing in wet cement, watching it dry around us. We do not like the feeling, but we step in it again and again. While life provides us a seemingly limitless supply of opportunity, we can also find a consistent barrage of obstacles that get in our way. They are like quicksand and roadblocks that pop up all around us; we are usually not prepared for what gets thrown our way. There are lots of ways to get stuck in life. Have you ever thought about all of the obstacles that you face?

A Worldwide Pandemic

Life is busy and full of noise. We are writing this book during a season where a lot of busyness and noise have been stripped away. Most of the time, this kind of shock to the system comes when we have had a major life event or shift, such as divorce, death, or a serious diagnosis. However, the current events of today have pushed the pause button on all of us. A worldwide pandemic is unavoidable. Setting aside any personal or political feelings, we can all agree on the reality that everyone has been impacted in many different ways, so no need to compare ourselves to anyone else. Some of us lost our concept of time, some of us lost our sense of normalcy. This season has accelerated the speed at which we internally reflect how we are showing up for our life. It has rearranged our priorities and exposed superficial behaviors in a very clarifying way.

It's no surprise that many of my clients were left to wonder if maybe they were depressed or had anxiety. During this time of COVID, there was a huge amount of isolation occurring, even from family and friends. There was also a lot of mindless binge-watching of tv or news and reckless eating. Inner dialogues began to rationalize these behaviors as "I have nothing else to do, so sleeping will work" and "I will do it later or tomorrow" became an acceptable response to activities that would actually create positive energy. Feeling depressed or feeling anxious about your life is a HUGE indicator that you are heading in the WRONG direction.

As this pandemic crisis waged war on our normalcy, we could begin to see our lives from a vastly different vantage point. Things that once mattered may no longer matter, and things that did not matter suddenly mean a lot to us. Again, this type of reflection isn't new, but it rarely happens to us all at the same time.

So, how are you feeling today? How has a worldwide pandemic impacted your life? Have you discovered anything new about yourself or about your life through this season? How has a pandemic made you feel STUCK?

Feeling Stuck

➡️ I feel board.

➡️ I'm so stuck… I don't know what to do.

➡️ I just don't have any energy to do things.

➡️ I know I am not doing the right things to feel better.

There are a multitude of reasons and circumstances that can block us from seeing beyond the horizon, that keep us from moving forward or turning on to a new road. For many of us, it's difficult enough to get through the day in front of us with all the responsibilities and tasks that pile up like laundry, overflowing email, and a sink full of dishes. Or perhaps all the space and energy you have allocated for each day is being siphoned by all the external forces you believe you have no control over. Maybe you've made a series of poor choices and assume you are now disqualified from having access to something greater for yourself. Or you're in the middle of a season of raising children to be decent human beings—which is no easy task, by the way—and you're just trying to keep your head above the waves. You haven't given much thought to wanting something more for your life.

All these things are true and real and may be unfolding in the story of your life. Some of these things are excuses; others are scars from past pains and failures. Regardless of where you are, if you have a burning in your soul, a desire that keeps resurfacing, please don't ignore it and think it will go away. Don't miss out on all the opportunities available to you if you only dared to dream. Don't miss the road less traveled, only to remain stuck in the same old holding patterns as before.

When we begin to lose our luster for life, when it becomes routine and predictable we subtly close ourselves off from interacting with the world. Things get small, we get small, we don't notice the drift off the highway. Now is the time to pull over and get out of the car to assess what the heck happened.

Land of the Familiar

We tend to stay in a familiar route we know, taking the easy way, with no desire to venture off or discover any new destinations. It can feel like human nature to live in a defined and limited space, to live with borders that are familiar to us. The land of the familiar is comfortable and safe. Our heart and mind are at ease, they don't need to work as hard when we recycle the same old habits and pathways. We get to turn down, or turn off, our navigation system and turn on the autopilot.

Although there are many benefits of autopilot, it can be a major factor to a stagnant and mediocre life. Autopilot makes it easy to fall into a rut. You become comfortable with taking your foot off the gas, hands no longer at ten and two, and eyes no longer on the road. Expectations are lowered, and at this moment, there's no need to reach for more. This momentary decision to use autopilot can turn into days, then weeks, months, and possibly even years. Every once in a while, you may have a day where a sighting of purpose or greatness shows up like a billboard directing you to make the next right, but you pass it by unwilling to disrupt the comfort of your current rhythm. Whether intentionally or unintentionally, you are making a decision to remain in the land of the familiar and continue on the autopilot's course. You have given up control of your direction and lost sight of your destination.

Are you stuck in a rhythm that's keeping you in a state of comfort rather than a state of growth? Think about the start of your week; imagine a typical Monday morning. You wake up feeling blah, unmotivated, overtaken by a negative fog. As you prepare to face another week, it just feels mundane, uninspiring, and filled with the sameness as the week before. Your days can begin with these feelings, but you don't have to stay there. I used to let these feelings have more power than they deserved, and guess what—they defined my choices for the day, which spilled over into my week. I'll be the first to say, the choices made out of stagnation and stuck did not help launch me into a future filled with the hope and promises of a purposeful life. How about you? How are you allowing the choices of today to dictate your tomorrow?

Here's a scenario that may hit close to home: Every morning and every night looks the same… "I wake up whenever I want and I go to sleep when I feel like it, usually when there's nothing to watch on TV. Then with the time in between, I fill in time hanging out on social media, getting something to eat, maybe texting a few friends, and sort of wandering about through the day without a plan. When I have a job, I fly out of bed because I didn't set the alarm, throw on some clothes from the day before (I didn't do the laundry), and hurry off. Since I arrived late, I'm feeling really embarrassed and tell myself I don't care, and pick up where I left off, counting down the hours to when I can go home. And that's it. I feel like I am on AUTOPILOT."

There it is, autopilot mode. Have you ever arrived somewhere and realized you don't remember the trip there, like the trip was just a blur? You could cruise through your day and never feel in control or ahead of what is happening around you. It is almost like you are standing still and the world just keeps spinning around you. Being on autopilot lessens the richness of our journey. Those stuck in this mode are usually filling time until something else happens, anticipating when things will end instead of preparing for new opportunities to begin. __ Put a check if this is you.

What do you think causes us to kill time or simply let it pass us by? When you find yourself drifting into autopilot, watching the clock, and waiting for the present to end, what is actually going through your mind? What is it about doing nothing that is so much better than trying to seize the moment? I've had to look at myself in the mirror and ask those questions, and I continue to wrestle with the answer. I know that autopilot is a cheaper way to travel, but it costs us our dreams, our joy, and our mission. There shouldn't be a season that we let go to waste. We shouldn't allow ourselves to outsource our life to mundane habits or serve a silent sentence of non-existence. God created you and me for more than that.

> Rise up; this matter is in your hands.
> We will support you, so take
> courage and do it.
>
> EZRA 10:4 (NIV)

Expert In Busyness

I closed my eyes and took a deep breath; when I opened them, I found myself curled up in the corner of my bedroom in a state of panic because I realized it was only Tuesday. How in the world am I supposed to make it through an entire week? I'm fairly certain my fuel tank is running on fumes at this point, and there's no filling station in sight. I was at a season of my life where I was a newly single mom of three. Three kids at three different schools because clearly, I planned that out well. I spaced them just far enough apart to be in elementary, middle, and high school at the same time. Yes, I agree; you would think that would have been enough of a load to handle for one day. Seriously, I was up at 5:00 a.m. to get the first one out the door because I thought it was my responsibility to make sure my 15-year-old had a nutritious meal to start his day: one down, two to go. I would constantly pray that everything ran smoothly. No forgotten lunches, no late buses, no missed alarms.

There was no room for error. I desperately needed it to run like a well-oiled machine, or I was crying in the corner by Tuesday. As you can imagine, there were a lot of tears on Tuesdays. The last drop-off was at 8:30 a.m.; I made it! Now I can take a nap. Just kidding… you didn't think I was serious, right?

Somewhere in the middle of alarm clocks, missing socks, unwashed gym clothes, misplaced homework, and burnt eggs— which are still nutritious, by the way—I was applying mascara and maybe some blush in an attempt to look presentable for the day. I had a job to get to because somebody had to put food on the table. The only way I survived the 24 hours in front of me was to break it up into three mini days. So, when everyone else at the office was saying their "have-a-good-evening" goodbyes, I was off to round three of my day: soccer practice, piano lessons, taxi rides galore at your service. These kids had places to go, people to see, and dreams to pursue, and I was the vehicle to make it happen.

I remember talking to my counselor about the time-management crisis I couldn't seem to escape. At the time, I couldn't fully connect why I felt so exhausted every week. Of course, I would rest on the weekends; and by rest, I mean laundry, meal prepping, putting in extra effort for quality time, more taxi service, soccer games, entertaining other mini-human beings that weren't my own so my kids could relish in their childhood. Anyway, I always prepared myself for a new week with a little pep talk I would compose from stringing together a series of the absolute best inspirational quotes *Pinterest* had to offer. So why did I hit a wall before I could even get going? She suggested I write down all the activities I do each day. That's where it clicked.

The list was way too long for any one person to sustain for even one day, let alone a week or perhaps several weeks. I knew I had to prioritize my time and energy, but all of these things felt like priorities. I didn't see any place where I could trim the fat. Not without feeling like I was an inadequate parent who didn't fully support all my kids' hobbies or the responsibilities that I had at home and at work. I chose to stay in this never-ending cycle of busyness.

Over time I got better at it, more efficient, less easily frazzled, but still tired. This was my life for what seemed like a never-ending season. By all accounts, I was busy. I was busy trying to be everything to everyone. I was busy trying to be the parent I didn't have growing up. I was busy trying to overcompensate for the poor judgment that landed me a spot in the divorced statistics. However, as busy as I was, there were some things that I had cut out of my life and was not making time for. I was not pursuing the dreams or desires of my heart. I was not caring for myself or allowing room for personal growth.

Busyness can display itself in many different forms. Sometimes when we are really busy, it feels as if life is moving too fast for us to keep up. Sometimes we have reasons to keep ourselves busy to avoid another issue or opportunity. And sometimes we find reasons and temptations to act busy or appear busy, as if we are attracted to the chaos and empowered by feeling overwhelmed. As a result, the more clutter and chaos we invite into our lives, the less time we will have to face the real challenges we are encountering deep down.

What season of life are you in? Perhaps you have landed a 40-hour gig where your passion and career align in perfect harmony. That's awesome! You can stop reading now… just kidding! For most of us, our chosen or landed-by-chance careers launch us into a frenzy-filled workday that provides us with productivity and a paycheck; however, when we leave the office for the day, we are left feeling unfulfilled and unsatisfied. The same can be true for stay at home parents. Our bodies ache for something more—a creative outlet, a way to feel alive and whole, a pathway to impact the world and people around us.

Let's take a deeper dive into busyness and uncover how it's altering the direction of your life.

busy·ness
/ˈbizēnəs/
noun
1: occupied with meaningless activity; the quality of being busy:
2: the state of having many details

According to the Merriam-Webster dictionary, the definition of busy is "occupied with meaningless activity." Busyness has become somewhat of an epidemic in our country. It is an addiction to which we are drawn and considered a symbol of honor to be celebrated and receive a gold star for. We are living in a world where the more our time is occupied, the more successful and impressive our lives are considered. We have a vision of what makes us successful, and we have been conditioned to believe this is true. The busier you are, the more productive you seem. So we simply begin to measure success based on the amount of time we don't have, regardless if we are actually pursuing anything of purpose.

Don't misunderstand me here. There are plenty of things we can be filling our time with, but do they **add** value to our lives? Does your version of busyness consist of important things that are pushing you towards your dreams and aspirations, or are they pulling you away from them?

We all have 24 hours in a day. Think about all the influential people in our lifetime. What sets them apart from you and me? Do you think they all waited until their schedules cleared before they began pursuing their path?

If you are serious about chasing your dream, you may want to consider making some changes to the busyness in your life. Overcommitting is not impressive; it is stressful. Busy doesn't necessarily mean impressive, and it certainly doesn't mean we are getting anything done. Wasteful busyness produces clutter and chaos to distract us from the dreams and aspirations bubbling inside, searching for a space to grow and evolve. When we stop to look back ten years from now, will our constant state of busyness leave us with an empty void of unfulfilled dreams and aspirations? If it is a better or happier life we are in search of, it's time to stop being torn in so many different directions that we lose sight of the dreams placed in our hearts leading us to where and who we were called to be.

Made the Wrong Turn

I was the first person in my family to graduate from college. Only people with a passion for helping the world would pursue a degree in social work. The base pay for a world changer in 1976 was surprisingly low and discouraging to face. And there was a fork in the road: one direction pursues a low earning career in social work, and the other opens up to a more lucrative but passionless job. Going against everything within me, I took a job that made really good money. It was never going to change the whole world, but it did change mine. Now I could afford to do more and live it up. But, slowly, the passion and fire to make a difference began to grow dim. That ONE big decision to make that turn completely changed the trajectory of my life for the next ten years; it was a long and spiraling journey down a one-way highway going nowhere fast. I was stuck in a lifestyle that was so far from the bright-eyed aspirations to help people in need; I couldn't recognize myself in the mirror. It was like being in the house of mirrors at a jamboree and needing to find your way out.

Have you ever been there? Well, that was me. Maybe you are there now; one big decision has taken you somewhere that you didn't intend to go. Or maybe you have made a million little decisions that have slowly led you away from where you started and now can't find your way back. Making decisions that go against who you are—your true self—will always make you feel LOST. The truth is, even if your wrong turn is lucrative, living outside of your true self is not where you want to stay.

_____ This is me; I have made some wrong turns.

Acknowledging that you made a wrong turn doesn't feel good at the time, but it can serve as a place for great change and motivation to flow in and move you in the direction you were meant to go. Whenever I get lost or stuck, I lean in and look up to God and ask for directions; He has the answers!

Unlearning Bad Habits

We all have some favorite sayings or catchphrases, right? Well, I know that I do. My kids often roll their eyes when they hear the classics coming out on repeat, but I keep going back to them because they are so good! A favorite saying of mine is, "You can't walk 10 miles into the forest and expect to get out in 5." Now, my kids have grown up in the suburbs, and the outdoors are unfamiliar, but I do believe they understand the purpose behind this phrase. Habits that have formed over a long period of time can take a long time to unlearn and change. A large decision to travel off course requires a large decision to get back on track.

To expand the margins for our dreams to prosper, we will need to take a closer look at some of the bad practices we have adopted—or inadvertently embraced—which are preventing us from putting our gifts and talents on display for the world to experience and benefit from. If you are feeling a bit introspective and brave, use a ✓ and identify areas needing some improvement.

_____ **#1 Excessive Screen time.** Are you scrolling social media in the morning and just before you sleep? How much time are you logging in these days? Excessive screen time removes you from being truly present with those around you and blocks you from focusing on the goals you have for your future. People turn to their devices when they are bored, as a time filler, or a coping habit to distract them from something they don't want to do. This form of escapism has the power to rob us of hours of time per day with very little positive energy. In fact, research shows it affects our moods, relationships, ability to concentrate on a deeper level of thinking, and disrupts sleep patterns over time. Screen addiction can be a real issue. If you want to get REAL about it, check your daily screen times for a week.

How much of that time could be utilized towards REAL LIFE activities you say you want to accomplish?

_____ **#2 Procrastination.** This is a habit and ritual of putting off things you "don't feel like doing," usually until the last minute. "Plenty of time; I will do that tomorrow." Tomorrow turns into days or weeks. "I'd rather be doing anything than this dreaded task." This habit results in us choosing convenience over commitment and distraction over discipline. Procrastination is the by-product of an unsettled root, and it needs to be pulled today.

> Following-through is the only thing
> that separates dreamers from people
> that accomplish great things.
>
> GENE HAYDEN

_____ **#3 Not setting your intentions.** You cannot hit the mark if you do not have a clear target. This literally means you are going to haphazardly fumble around, hoping you get a few things done AND probably miss the most important things. Quite simply, it is extremely difficult to get the most out of a meeting, a schedule, a relationship, or a season of life when there are no clear intentions. We may have goals or intentions, but if they are not firmly set by practice and shared, then we will most often experience disappointment; we will feel like our time has been wasted.

_____ **#4 Perfectionism.** A pursuit of excellence is healthy, but perfectionism can be a curse and a crutch. "I have to get it just right; it has to be perfect." This may sound admirable, but it can lead to a breakdown under the heavy burden we place upon ourselves. Or, it can cause a form of paralysis when we can't move forward because it will never be ready or good enough. I know a thing or two about this. For most of my adult life, I viewed it as one of my strengths. I often saw it as a positive trait that would undoubtedly lead to great success — a healthy behavior of setting high standards that would motivate me to be the best version of myself.

Throughout my college career, I knew I would need to allocate more time when I had a project or paper due. Not only because I was an undergraduate while raising three kids, but because it would take me 30 minutes to formulate two sentences. So I created space for my perfectionism to flourish by staying up late, getting up early, agonizing over a single paragraph for days longer than any of my peers, studying for exams for weeks and weeks because the thought of missing one question was more stressful to me than the extra time I would need to put in. And if you thought that was the extent of my extremism, my home had to be spotless, my kids well-groomed, and I was the glue that held my unstable marriage together.

I was not aware of the depth of this problem until the day I found myself in my doctor's office pulling my hair back to show him "the most impressive" bald spot he's ever seen. Imagine a shiny, light-reflective, hairless patch the size of a silver dollar. That's what we are talking about here. I told him if I'm going to do something, I'm going to do it well, and this was certainly one more piece of evidence to prove it. Even in my baldness, I had to be perfect. As only I would expect, I graduated from college magna cum laude, but it came at the price of my health. I started paying more attention to some other ways my perfectionist tendencies were costing me. I noticed how I would set goals but not make any moves until I knew I could complete them perfectly. Years and years went by, and there was no forward movement towards any sort of future progress. I remained in the same spot year after year, paralyzed by the need to be perfect.

Brené Brown, a writer and research professor at the University of Houston Graduate College of Social Work, distinguishes between perfectionism and healthy behavior. She says, "Perfectionism is not the same thing as striving to be your best. Perfection is not about healthy achievement and growth." She explains that perfectionism is used by many people as a shield to protect against the pain of blame, judgment, or shame. Perhaps you struggle with perfectionism, but have you ever considered why? No matter how you got here, it is time to build healthier habits.

_____ **#5 Negative Relationships.** We are meant to be connected; you are worth knowing and loving. And yet, some relationships are just draining. You just got off the phone with one of your "friends," and you feel blah, unmotivated, down, and maybe irritated. Maybe your family situation isn't supportive, and well, what are you supposed to do about your interactions with them? They're your family. Although these relationships are really important to you, are they a positive or negative source of energy in your life? And if it's the latter, the real dilemma is what are you going to do about it. How can you cut out your best friend of 10 years or your family? Have you ever left an encounter and thought to yourself, "Wow, that was draining?"

_____ **#6 People-Pleasing.** Do you find yourself saying "yes" to everyone? Are you doing so many things for others at home or at work that you are stressed and frantic by the end of the day because you didn't get to things you needed to get done? The BIG message you are saying to yourself is your time, energy, and passion is worth less than everyone else's, and your worth and value come from the approval of others. People-pleasing is a habit we learn. People love you, but at the end of the day, do you love yourself? It's hard to set healthy boundaries for yourself if you are a known people pleaser. Do you find yourself saying, "I will get to my things later," and then find yourself working past midnight and neglecting your family? Does saying yes to everyone else get you to where you want to be in your future? Start saying YES TO YOU!

_____ **#7 Substance USE.** Maybe you don't have an addiction to alcohol or drugs, but maybe you have a few beers or glasses of wine each night and don't see anything wrong with that. But honestly, after you have a drink, do you really feel like working on the things that you said are important to you, like working out, writing, setting your intention list for the next day to be successful. OR do you blow off the rest of the evening and then wake up late and play catch up the next day?? Ouch, maybe this hurts. All evidence from years of research suggests there is a negative impact of alcohol's effects on our brain and body functions on a short and long-term basis. Even if you don't feel like your use is out of control, maybe it's becoming a regular habit taking you away from your efforts of becoming a better version of yourself. Give it up for a few days and see for yourself!!

If you used your pen to make a ✓ on any of the time robbers, you've got a time and energy leak working against you.

The good news is YOU can change all this and more!

The question we have to ask ourselves is, how is this habit serving me? Is being a people pleaser, hanging out with the wrong crew, sucking down a beer, not having a plan for your day with your face in the phone really who you want to be?

Being stuck doesn't have to be where you stay.

Breaking the Habit Challenge

Pick one habit from the list above. This is a habit that you will begin to tackle, commit to, and grow beyond. Write that habit here:

_____

Why did you pick this habit? Write down your thoughts and feelings about how this habit has impacted you and what you will gain by breaking through it.

_____

_____

_____

_____

We have been stuck between a rock and a hard place. We lost our way, and tragically, our tools and habits are only making things worse. When we begin to remove bad habits and build better ones, we begin to free ourselves from being stuck. Now we are going to get to the good stuff. Take a posture of openness for the next chapter, open heart, open mind, open eyes, and open ears because there might just be something for you! When we grow, we flourish.

Getting UNSTUCK is a process for sure. Have you ever been stuck somewhere? I sure have! On a visit to Africa, we were in an open-air Serengeti vehicle where we experienced the sights and sounds of the wild up close. The topography there is hilly and rough with deep gullies, and sometimes they are full of water from rain. The problem is you don't know how deep it is until you go into it. The one we went through was so deep that the truck got stuck. We knew we were stuck, and it wasn't going to be a simple rocking back and forth process to get out. There was a lot of trial and error, trying different ideas, pushing, moving rocks, jamming on the gas and then the brakes, and also keeping an eye out for any large animals that might have been looking for lunch! So, it's not a one-and-done deal. Our focus was to get the vehicle from being stuck and working that out until it happened. That's the challenge for you, to figure out how to start getting unstuck and finding the one thing that can help get you out of that ditch. As you begin to focus on doing that, your mindset will begin to open up, grow, and change. So buckle up as you are on your own Serengeti trip in life, moving away from your old stuck place. Say goodbye to that!

You are **HERE**
taking inventory of your life.

You are **HERE**
inviting in new energy.

You are **HERE**
breaking free from bad habits.

You are **HERE**
motivated to pursue greater things.

THE MAKING OF A MINDSET

Hopefully, you have a better understanding of how you became STUCK. Despite what muddy puddle, pothole, or deep trench you may be finding yourself in at this very minute, we have no intention of leaving you there. The way out is through, and the way through is changing how you think, speak to yourself, and envision a future life full of all the hopes, possibilities, and dreams waiting to be released by you. Guess who's responsible for creating and finding the dream that will begin to put it all together?

You are the architect of your life.

Assessing your dreams is about finding your purpose. Our purpose was designed to fulfill and bring vivid color to the places and spaces surrounding us. Everyone's journey is different, and yet we are all trying to get to the same destination—living out our dreams and abiding in our purpose. With a dream-killer mindset, you will never get there. You will keep circling around and around, buffering your time away. Longing for a better, more fulfilled life will not be enough to get you across the finish line; it isn't enough just to want it. This type of work requires the same level of commitment one would apply when setting out to watch a ten-season series on your favorite streaming platform. It demands some serious dedication and focus. So let's begin building a foundation that can withstand any hurdle that may come our way. If you are craving a more satisfying, on purpose, and abundant life, then commit to making the necessary changes to put you on the most favorable path.

> This means that anyone who belongs to Christ has become a new person. The old life is gone; a new life has begun!

2 CORINTHIANS 5:17 (NLT)

You Are Here. It is time to change your mindset. Changing your mindset is a must to discovering and living a life of purpose and fulfillment. Thank God we are able to renew our minds, re-work the programming and change the direction of our life. Now you get to leverage your history to build your new future.

Here's a quick snapshot of the different ways we view the world according to our filter.

STUCK Mindset   vs.   GROWTH Mindset

STUCK Mindset	GROWTH Mindset
Skeptical & Fixed Mindset	Optimism & Open to Growth
Limiting Beliefs/Life History	New Narrative, New State
Autopilot/Default Thinking	Deliberate & Intentional
Shame-Won't happen for me	Positive Affirmations
Lost/Hopelessness	Gratitude

Busyness	Prioritizing/ Time Management
Bad Habits/Complacency	Deliberate Thinking

As a certified life coach, I have listened to endless hours of experts sharing their thoughts on the importance of changing your state of mind. Our state of mind controls every thought, emotion, and feeling. Think about your state of mind as the sail of a boat. The smallest degree of shift will alter each decision, which will alter each step, which will alter each outcome. Shifting your state of mind holds the power to change the trajectory of your life. This is why it's important to view our minds as muscles that need to be developed and strengthened. Here are some questions to get you started.

Are your thoughts, feelings, and emotions moving you forward? Do they serve you well, or are they holding you back? Are you flexible enough to shift direction when met with challenges, or do you freeze or try to bulldoze your way through?

The road ahead will require many stops and many turns. Navigating the paths of life and successfully moving towards our hopes and dreams will require us to work on our mindset. Earlier in this book, we introduced the importance of our mindset. We began with the difference between a fixed mindset and a growth mindset, which ultimately is the difference between believing that our future can be brighter than our past. From that foundation, we branch out away from limiting beliefs and towards newer and better stories that we can tell ourselves. We turn off the autopilot and begin to think about our journey through life with more intention and care. We drop the bitter fruit of shame and grab hold of positive and sweet affirmations—we can do this! Slowly, bad habits fade in our rearview mirror as we prioritize our time and bring better tools to help us succeed. Ultimately, we are no longer feeling lost when we embrace a new mindset. We have work to do, ground to gain, and many stops and turns to get us back on track. But isn't it sweet to know that we can do this? Our dreams and ambitions are ready and waiting for us.

In this chapter, we are going to break down seven stops you will need to make and identify which way to turn. Each of these will help shift your mindset to get you back on track in your journey through life.

➡ 1st Stop: Be Open and Desire to Grow Forward

At this first stop, we need to pause to acknowledge that our mind is either opened or closed. We know that you intuitively understand that an open mind is healthier and happier than a closed mind, but that doesn't mean this turn is easy. Many of us believe that keeping our hearts tightly tethered to the familiar allows us to walk the safest path, free from failure, risk, and any disappointments that could be waiting just around the corner. If we keep our path just narrow enough, there is less room for our inadequacies and imperfections to show through. However, narrow also means there's not a whole lot of room to encounter growth. Let's turn towards growth and embrace what's ahead.

Take a baby step right now. Own your current mindset, get real with it, and acknowledge how it has played an influential part in your lack of success and fulfillment. As you reflect at this stop, understand that you are not what is lacking, you are not inadequate; you've just approached life with an out-of-date mindset, and it has been holding you back for far too long. It has locked you in place without you even knowing it! A growth mindset embraces a willingness to learn more about yourself, what you want to do in life by welcoming challenges, being positive and confident, working through obstacles, having an "all-in" effort, inviting uncertainty, and being open to feedback to grow. Here are some ways to redirect how you think:

➡ Build a habit of daily affirmations of your worth and potential.

➡ Visualize your dreams and opportunities, focus on your growth.

➡ Make a list of things you would start doing that you were pushing off before.

➡ Pray for an open mind and heart to clarify your intended purpose in life.

➡ Find hope and believe there is a purpose and a plan for your life.

➡ 2nd Stop: Loosen Limiting Beliefs

At this stop, we need to work on our limiting beliefs. These are the stories that we tell ourselves that cause us to hit the breaks when we should be hitting the gas. In chapter 2, you defined your limiting beliefs. Take a moment to write out some of your recent or current limiting beliefs about yourself or your life.

My limiting beliefs about myself are:

_____

Who told you those things? Where did those beliefs come from?

_____

Changing our mindset from old to new is what creates freedom and injects new energy into our otherwise stuck lives. It can put you on a new highway full of wide-open lanes. It's time to define your new narrative, to define what you now believe about yourself. You get to decide if you want those old limiting beliefs to keep running your life or if you want to be in control with a fresh new view of things. Whenever you clear out "old" things in your home and replace them with something new, don't you feel better and different about your room when you walk in? Just like you made decisions about making those updates, you can make new ones regarding what you believe about yourself!

> For you created my inner being; you
> knit me together in my mother's womb.
> I praise you because I am fearfully and
> wonderfully made; your works are
> wonderful, I know that full well.

PSALM 139:13-14 (NIV)

When we read through the Bible, there are some amazing things that God says about you and about me. Sometimes I wonder and reflect on what the next moment of my life would look like if I fully embraced those beliefs. If I am known and loved, forgiven and accepted, wonderfully made and purposed by God, empowered and invited to do great things—then by the goodness and grace of God, I can be more and do more than I realize. I can reach higher and dream bigger than I would when I am bound by my limiting beliefs.

Take a moment to now write out a few new beliefs about yourself and about your life. Try writing a new belief for all of the limiting beliefs that you wrote earlier, a statement that fills your heart with peace and joy.

_____

_____

_____

➡ 3rd Stop: From a Default to a Deliberate Mindset

Reflecting at our third stop, we need to make a crucial adjustment and turn. We cannot move forward or grow beyond our current circumstances if we remain on autopilot. Studies show that "46.9% of the day we are in autopilot mode." What do you think about this statistic which suggests that roughly half of your day simply happens with little to no intention or deliberate effort?

Some autopilot action is harmless, but staying in that zone for too long will have many negative consequences. We have a "predictor" in our brains called the Reticular Activating System. Its purpose is to protect us from harm, and it's generally based on our old programming and limiting beliefs. Your mind will contemplate all the worst-case scenarios and why you shouldn't try to do something big. Your dreaming can easily be shut down here without much effort. Your autopilot will naturally direct you to what is safe and familiar, avoiding new or unknown paths. Most dreams and ambitions are tremendously unknown and new, and your autopilot mode is going to resist it.

This programming keeps us stuck and reroutes us time after time into old patterns and behaviors. Every one of us was wired for greatness in our own way. We were created to create and cultivate a lifestyle true to our purpose and passion in life. Try to identify several examples and areas of your life that have been stuck in default mode.

Write them down here:

_____

_____

_____

In a deliberate mode of processing, YOU are present for yourself and controlling what you think about and what you do. Believing you can do it, being strong-minded, optimistic, and positive will begin moving you forward, gaining momentum and confidence every step of the way. Bring intentionality to your day and into each moment of opportunity. Think through what is before you, prepare for it, and take the proper action steps to make the most out of it. Pick one or two examples or areas that you identified as default areas, write out what a more deliberate approach to the situation or opportunity could look like:

_____

_____

_____

> Whatever things are true, whatever is noble, whatever is right, whatever is pure, whatever is lovely, whatever is admirable—if anything is excellent or praiseworthy—think about such things.

PHILIPPIANS 4:8 (NIV)

4th Stop: Strengthen Self-Esteem

Three stops down, we are making progress and covering a lot of ground. All of these stops matter, and the fourth stop is no different. Our self-esteem is like the fuel that our engine runs on. Low self-esteem means we are running dangerously close to empty and are not going to travel as far or as freely as we ought to. We need to constantly measure our heart and make sure that we are filling up and strengthening our self-esteem. So let's take time at this stop to check where we are today and explore a few ways to fill up our tank with a healthy dose of fuel.

Does your current view of yourself sound like one or more of these?

➡️ "Nothing's ever worked out for me, no matter what I do."

➡️ "I don't deserve it; I've screwed up too much."

➡️ "I have nothing to offer; how could someone like me do something like that?"

Just think of how many times you have spoken those things about yourself?

You are negatively affirming nothing good can come from your life; and eventually, you will believe it and start living a life in alignment with what you believe to be true. No matter when it started for you, it's time to change your programming. I don't believe any of us are opposed to having high self-esteem. Most of us can identify the value of improving our self-worth; however, if this task were easy, I'd be rocking the jacket that's been in the back of my closet for the last several decades! Newsflash, there is not one of us here on this planet who will make it through life unscathed by rejection, failure, betrayal, humiliation, or any of the other emotional wounds we will press up against in our lifetime. But, how we respond to these encounters will dictate the terms of our future.

Brain scan studies demonstrate that when our self-esteem is higher, we are likely to experience common emotional wounds such as rejection and failure as less painful and bounce back from them more quickly. When our self-esteem is higher, we are also less vulnerable to anxiety.

GUY WINCH

Imagine if you could wave a magic wand of "I am" statements, and voila, you will never again have to experience the residual pain of old emotional wounds. Now drop your imagination like it's a hot potato and come back into the reality that improving your self-esteem is going to require a little bit of work. Developing healthier emotional habits must be met with intentional effort, but I can promise you the return on this investment will be well worth all your efforts! With a full tank of healthy and happy self-esteem, you will travel further and faster than you ever have before.

How do you build your self-esteem? Great question! Here are intentional action steps and reflections for filling up on the good stuff to strengthen your heart and mind:

➡️ Improve your physical health. Your mind and body work together. Exercise, drink lots of water, get good rest, and talk with a physician.

➡️ Focus on things you are good at, continue to grow and develop in those areas.

➡️ Take on challenges. Saying "yes" will expand your growth.

➡️ Decrease self-criticism and increase self-love and compassion.

➡️ Accept compliments!

➡️ Make a list of all the good qualities you possess.

For most of my life, I considered myself a fairly optimistic, high-esteem, confident person. A few years ago, I challenged myself to really pay close attention to how I talked to myself. During this very intentional observation period, I noticed that I used the word "just" a lot. And by a lot, I mean I used it as an adjective to describe *just* about everything. It seems pretty harmless, right? I'm *just* going to run to the store; I *just* need to get more sleep; I worked out for *just* 30 minutes; it was *just* a 200-hour yoga teacher training certification. What I realized was I was using this four-letter word to minimize the small things AND the big things as if they held the same weight. The moment I practiced removing this word from my vocabulary was the moment my confidence and self-esteem strengthened to a new level. It was not *just* a 200-hour yoga teacher training; it was something

I dedicated myself to for several months to gain a deeper level of understanding and expertise so I could help others.

Choose one from the above list, circle it, and begin practicing it until it becomes ingrained in the deepest parts of your soul. If you find yourself lacking positive words, the internet is full of affirmations and empowering beliefs. Pick one, any one that resonates with who you are or who you desire to become; then wash, rinse, and repeat. It may take a hundred million times before you actually believe it, and that's because you have to counter the hundred million times you spoke in opposition to this new belief. Claim back the power over your life by building your self-esteem and shedding shame so you can begin to walk more confidently towards your goals. Be committed to trying these action steps; they will make a profound difference in your life and propel you to new heights as you journey forward.

➡ 5th Stop: Dazed and Confused

At this fifth stop, we need to acknowledge how foggy and disorienting the journey through life can be. There are times when we look around and realize that we are in an unfamiliar place, and we are not confident where to turn next. You still know what your destination is, but the current location and path forward has left you feeling dazed and confused. You feel a pit in your stomach. Finding yourself in the land of the unknown can make us feel vulnerable, insecure, discouraged, and lost; those feelings can come in all shapes and sizes.

Maybe this feeling surfaced as a result of a loved one passing away, a relationship ending, or you were overlooked for a promotion. You had a vision and an idea of where you were and what was coming next when suddenly everything is turned around, and life has taken you in a new direction. Or perhaps you are feeling aimless, floating from one thing to the next, and there has not been much intention or direction in your life for quite some time. Experiences and emotions have muddled your life, causing you to lose your sense of direction and purpose.

It is time for a new mindset; it is time for new clarity and direction. This may feel daunting and hard to digest, but we promise you this is a golden opportunity to recapture hope and peace. You can dream and envision a new horizon with vibrant colors and details, a joyful road to travel forward, and a secure destination to move towards. The fog will clear, the path will illuminate. We cannot change the landscape of where we are today, but we do not have to stay there. We can move with purpose and intention.

> You do not need to know precisely
> what is happening or exactly where it is
> all going. What you need is to recognize
> the possibilities and challenges offered
> by the present moment, and to embrace
> them with courage, faith, and hope.
>
> THOMAS MERTON

When we are feeling dazed and confused, these action steps can help us move from lost to found:

➡ Try another direction. If you keep coming back to the same place, try something new, think outside of the box with courage, faith, and hope.

➡ Use your compass. Establish core values and know them well. Principles and values are even better than directions because they are always true.

➡ Pray. Do not be heavy burdened, panicked, or discouraged. Bring all of your requests to God and seek out His peace and wisdom.

➡️ Find sources of hope and courage. Build up faith in God, yourself, your dreams, and your passions. Hope and courage can come from a multitude of places. Lean in and fill up.

➡️ Ask for help from a trusted source. You are not alone. While not everyone is in a position to help (you don't want to ask someone who is lost for directions), there are many potential sources of help who can walk and talk you through the fog.

Let's reflect more on these action steps and answer some questions:

Write the names of a few people who are cheering you on:

_____

_____

What's your internal compass/core values?

_____

_____

_____

Where does your source of hope and belief for your future come from?

_____

_____

➡ 6th Stop: Choose Your Busyness

How you spent the last 24 hours is a good indicator of the direction your life is headed. John Maxwell was onto something when he said that the secret to your success is determined by your daily agenda. If you don't prioritize what is important to you and map it out daily/weekly, there is a 100 percent chance you will never move the needle from where you currently are to where you want to be in life. With so many distractions every day, prioritizing has to be a PRIORITY! A lack of this skill set will allow your days to own you instead of you owning your day. Here's a quick way to get started with having less stress and more productive days ahead.

Prioritizing allows you to gain traction. This requires you to develop a new mindset in the arena of time management and scheduling. Take the challenge to work through these steps. Find a place to write your responses where you will easily see and monitor them.

#1 List your top 3 priorities—three important action steps that you will commit time and energy to because they will help you move forward and not just fill empty space. Use your deliberate thinking and focus on your future!

#2 Create a time log for one week to see how you are spending your time each day.

#3 Go back over your log and tally up the time you spent on those top 3 priorities.

#4 How did you do? Did you spend as much time on your top action steps as you should? How did your time compare with other activities like social media or other draining activities?

#5 Reassess and set goals for next week. Do you need to aim for more time or less time in any area? Do you need to adjust your top priorities at all? Again, use your deliberate thinking and focus on your future when considering your priorities.

There is a good chance that simply tracking your time helps you become more focused and disciplined throughout the week, giving you more time to focus on what matters the most.

Being busy is something most of us will need to spend some due diligence managing. Because being busy with the right things takes intentional practice. You may already feel like you are super productive with your days. By all accounts, this may be true. But are you pointing that productivity in the direction of your dreams? Is there some trimming and pruning you need to do to create space where your dream will grow? Something I quickly noticed when I began pursuing my dream was that I had only so much time available in my day, and I had to be really selective with how I was going to spend it. I am a single parent, which means my days carry the risk of being overtaken by the plans of other human beings. I have a full-time job; as a result, eight hours of my day are spent bringing home the bacon. Instead of sitting around hoping I could steal a few hours each day, I developed a plan to ensure my busyness was focused in the direction of my dream. Prioritizing and clearing the space to follow through with specific action steps is the key to advancing your vision.

➡ 7th Stop: Clearing the Queue

At this seventh stop, we get to leave our bad habits behind us. Breaking bad habits is just as important as developing good ones. Your good habits allow you to build momentum towards whatever dream or goal is ahead. However, if you squeeze a few healthy habits into your day and fail to eliminate the bad ones, it will feel like you're spinning your wheels in the mud, unable to gain any real traction. Amy Morin, a licensed mental health counselor, has worked with thousands of people who felt stuck. After much studying at a deeper level, she discovered that "people who persevere in life didn't just have healthy habits—they were also intentional about avoiding unhealthy habits that would keep them stuck." According to her observations, "those who were intent on reaching their greatest potential refused to indulge in counterproductive bad habits. Meaning the key to their progress wasn't just what they did. It was more what they didn't do."

> If your habits don't line up with your
> dream, then you need to either change
> your habits or change your dream.
>
> JOHN C MAXWELL

Can you think of any bad habits that might be getting in your way or slowing you down in the pursuit of your dream? You are here, meaning you want to change your life. Your next step is to get honest with yourself and commit to eliminating the bad habits keeping you from your future self. Depending on the scope of your habits, you may want to get some help by setting up a system of accountability either from friends, family, or seeking professional help.

The Almighty Power of ACCOUNTABILITY

You know your life is supposed to be so much more than what it is right now. You may be feeling very alone in all of that, down on yourself, anxious, or don't have a clue of what to do. There's a sense of hopelessness, which can be heavy. It's as if you are down in a dark pit looking up; there is just a little bit of light coming in, just enough to keep looking up. Surely there has got to be a way to get out.

God wired us to be dependent on Him to fulfill our ambitious dreams. He created us and inspired us to exist. He did not create us to be or feel alone. We all need His help to navigate life and purpose. And God created us to help each other, so we need help from others to move forward and grow as well. Perhaps in the past you haven't been able to get where you wanted to go, or maybe you never even tried. If you are operating with a fixed mindset, then you probably are not looking for help, and any voice of accountability goes in one ear and out the other. Accountability is NOT having someone telling you what to do or what you did wrong. An authentic accountability relationship is about the process of empowering you to do what you say YOU want to accomplish! There is a purpose and a plan mapped out that you are in agreement with and committed to with someone whom you trust and believe can help you succeed in your goals. It's about being willing to learn and grow when you fall short and celebrate when you achieve success. Accountability requires a growth mindset and vulnerability. These will all work to your advantage. Once you have committed to your plan and your reasons, adding a layer of accountability with someone who cares and wants to see you cross the finish line can give you the extra motivation to keep taking those baby steps when you don't feel like it!

Believe, have faith, and it will happen!

It was a huge step of faith when we first decided to write this book. We signed an official paid contract with our publishing company, and it quickly became real, fun, and scary all at the same time. Then our publisher told us we had to tell people what we were up to right NOW. Eeks! I wish I had a selfie of our shocking facial expressions. What do you mean now? We are introverts. We are going to need more time to process this! That kind of exposure really tested our faith and belief. That old programming—doubt, fear of a flop, what people would think; you know, that old default thinking—began to flood in. And by the way, we have done a lot of self-improvement work; years and years of very intentional, lying on the therapist couch, tears flowing, mind-exhausting kind of work to reprogram the limiting beliefs, negative self-talk, and story we have been telling ourselves.

After much soul searching and many sleepless nights, we were walking with new-found confidence, stronger belief, and a fresh perspective on the goodness of God and the blessings that He continuously offers. It was a bigger vision than either of us could have ever imagined. We had come a LOOONG way from the day when we first believed we were destined to give up all our hopes and dreams for an abundant future. Yet, in our humanness, it is not always enough to keep all the old behaviors and thought processes from resurfacing and trying to pull us back into an old familiar version of ourselves. The old programming will flood in. Put it in your "to be expected" file so you can prepare yourself for when it does. While a new, improved version of yourself will provide the best platform to achieve desirable results, better doesn't mean it will be a smooth paved road free from any deer darting in your path. You are pursuing something you once thought impossible. You are clearing a different path and establishing new habits with a new mindset. With accountability, you can remain strong and resolve to keep going, especially when old habits try to creep back into your life.

Once we stepped out and told a few people about our book, it reinforced our new mindset. The trust of speaking our goals and dreams out loud to other people made our belief about our future even stronger. It's only when YOU ARE HERE, reaching the first of many lookout points where you can see where you came from and where you are headed. Each stop offers an opportunity to reinforce a healthy mindset and strengthen your foundation so you are prepared to grow stronger and be more equipped for the future ahead. Your destination is to dream! The BEST of you is right around the corner!

You are **HERE**
developing a deliberate mindset.

You are **HERE**
clearing the space for the
new you to emerge.

You are **HERE**
ready to awaken your heart again.

You are **HERE**
ready to step into your true self!

PART 2

BUILDING
YOUR
DREAMS

YOU WERE CREATED TO CREATE

chapter five

The Best of You Is Waiting to Be Discovered

We were all created to DREAM, to create something in this world, to make a difference. Dreaming is an innate ability. We are all purposefully and specifically wired with the desire to crave the absolute best life has to offer. Ultimately, our fulfillment is designed to impact the world around us, and we will! It is in the pursuit of our dreams that we uncover the greatest parts of ourselves. YET... So many of us forfeit the value of our dreams for a predictable routine. Many of us were not encouraged to dream, or we trade them in at below market value for a life of certainty. Since we have captured your attention for at least the rest of this chapter, we want you to know that there is a dream made especially for YOU! Seriously, it was designed with your specific skills, talents, and capabilities in mind.

Dreams come a size too big
so we can grow into them.

JOSIE BISSET

Can you even begin to believe that? There is no better day than today to identify, develop, or rediscover your dream.

As a little kid, I distinctly remember waking up every day with

a pep-in-my-step type of excitement for all the opportunities and
exploration that was awaiting me. My only requirement was to
show up ready for an adventure. My imagination was filled to the
brim with all the things I was capable of and talented in. I dreamed
I could climb to the very top of what I perceived to be the largest
oak tree in the existence of the entire world, and so I did! Step by
step, my freckle-faced, pony-tailed, petitely designed self set a goal
and turned it into a reality. There were no "what if I didn't make
it to the top" doubts or "what if I DID make it to the top" fears!
Those words, this thought process, this style of reasoning was never
a part of our original dialogue. I could have easily assumed that I
would get stuck up there, and some squirrels would use my face as
target practice for their empty acorn shells. But at that time, no such
thought entered my mind.

I was a born dreamer. My imagination had a way of running
wild and free and had a careless tune about it. I could stay stuck in
my head for days at a time and be perfectly content and happy, never
looking out to see what was going on with the rest of the world. I
loved it there. It was safe, and I could create whatever reality my little
heart desired. As the story of my life took a turn, it caused a shift
for my once inquisitive, imaginative, investigative sense of self. This
natural disposition was replaced with a more logical, crisis-handling,
independent self in survival mode. I was no longer operating
carelessly and free because, at the ripe young age of 15, I was now
responsible for other human beings. As I became an adult overnight
and was forced to rise to the occasion, something overtook my "you

can do anything you want and don't let anyone tell you otherwise" attitude towards life. The longer this carried on, the more ingrained it became.

Eventually, my desire to dream of greater things was eroded to an unrecognizable whisper. I started operating out of fear and liability. All risk was now eliminated from my decision-making process because who was I to jeopardize other people's livelihoods? Putting dinner on the table and making sure basic needs were met was possible if I would just play it safe. This carried through into my twenties and thirties. I no longer believed pursuing my calling was available to me because I let the waves of life pound against my belief system. And so, just like many before me, I started directing my energy to accept this lot in life. Soon I could no longer hear even the whisper of a dream. I told myself if I was a good mom and my kids turned out ok, then well, that was good enough for me. And it truly would have been. But even so, there were days, hours, and moments I couldn't help wondering, what if this wasn't all that was meant for me? What if my story was much bigger than the limitations I was placing on myself? What if your story is too? I was ready to discover more, to nurture the BEST in me.

> You are not here merely to make a living, you are here in order to enable the world to live more amply, with greater vision, with a finer spirit of hope and achievement. You are here to enrich the world, and you impoverish yourself if you forget the errand.
>
> WOODROW WILSON

Divinely Appointed

- You were created to create value in your life and for the world.
- To create, we must discover what we were created for.
- To create, we must dream about possibilities.
- To create, we must track down the divine purpose for our life.

Once you start to move towards your divine purpose, everything will begin to change. Then it all comes together and makes sense. How you think, what you do, what you wear, how you are motivated, and everything within you starts to hone in on that target and propel you forward. Your body, mind, and spirit are hard-wired to align and move in the direction of that purpose.

Dreaming is ultimately about awakening. The unconscious, from which dreams bubble up, seems to contain an image of the way you're supposed to be, and continually works toward the expression of this potential, day and night.

GREGG LEVOY

Dreams are the longings that rise into our awareness when we allow ourselves to imagine what seems impossible to our logical minds. It is alive, gives you energy, fills your soul; it's part of your life adventure. Think back on a moment where you felt good about yourself, and you were doing things that were important and mattered to you and to others. God created you to dream. God is inviting you to be creative as you fulfill your purpose. When you walk in the direction of your dream, you begin aligning with your most authentic self, your designed and appointed self. The dream becomes the vision of YOUR unique purpose.

There have been many authors and scholars attempting to streamline exactly what it means to pursue your dream. With so much interchangeable terminology, it's no wonder we get confused. A dream for your life is not about daydreaming, or a pipedream not based on probability, or living your dreams vicariously through others, or career-oriented ideas.

A dream is an inspiring picture of a future that energizes your mind, will, and emotions, empowering you to do everything you can to achieve it. A dream worth pursuing is a picture and blueprint of a person's purpose and potential.

JOHN MAXWELL

Your dream is important! Dreams are an indicator of what you already know about something. It is a stirring in your soul that carries your thoughts, feelings, and purpose for your life. Without a dream, we are left walking aimlessly. Dreams show up in our lives to guide us towards areas we need growth and development. They are like a compass that will help guide us to our desired destination. If we only understood why dreaming was so important to the story of our lives, we wouldn't skip this page thinking it didn't apply to us. Without them, we are left to settle for a stale mediocrity of going through the motions of life but not really experiencing the depth of what is available to us if we pushed just beyond the next door.

Open the door to your dreams. It is up to you to pursue them!

Find Your Moment Of Knowing

How will you know when something is shifting? Are you hearing that small internal voice tugging? Do you feel like you need to be doing something different? You could be in a job where you're doing ok, but maybe you've plateaued, reached your goal, or hunger for another one. Perhaps you thought you'd reached your final destination but came to realize you have a desire to go further. Could it be that you are in a season of change? Your kids have moved out, and space and time that was once filled with the cluttered chaos of getting three kids off to three different schools hoping you didn't forget someone somewhere, soccer practice, dance lessons, piano lessons, skateboarding camps, friends' sleep-overs, and oh yeah, you also have to feed them, water them, make sure they have clean clothes to wear, shoes that fit, and the list goes on and on; this space is now suddenly empty, and the sense of purpose that once served you no longer exists in the same way.

You didn't start off not dreaming, not believing you were made for more. No matter how modest of a background you came from, what parenting style our parents used, what type of clothes you wore, or how many friends you had, every one of us was born with the innate wiring to do great things. I was made for greatness, and guess what, so were you! In his book, "The Greatest You," Trent Shelton's inspiration to us is that we were all made for greatness and we were "created on purpose, for a purpose." Did you know we all have access to greatness? If we can do it, you can too! No one is exempt or underqualified. Wherever you find yourself today, begin believing and find something that truly inspires you and gives meaning to your life. We can go through this life we were afforded, either simply being alive or choosing to create a life worth living.

The best way to enrich your life is to invite meaning and purpose into it, and dreaming big is how to do it. Having a goal and figuring out how to make it a reality will bring a richness to your life that will not only benefit you but will also spill over into the world around you. It is in the discovery and chasing of a dream where you will begin to figure out and shape what you actually want from life. Oftentimes we are put on unintended paths out of the desire to fill someone else's needs or expectations. Or not knowing what our path is due to a lack of exploration. We may have been so caught up in the momentum we forgot to ask ourselves what we need. Too many of us fall into a skeptical mindset where inspiration, new energy, and never-before-considered goals seem to be as distant as your cousin, who never calls or shows up to family events. There is NO age limit on following your dream; so whether you are in your early twenties or late seventies, it is never too late to step onto a path of purpose that will motivate and illuminate a new you.

It's your choice which way you decide to go in life. Make a decision today.

If you want to continue living a life of feeling stuck and stagnant, then you have made your decision. If you are curious and tired of the life you've been living and ready to make a change because you KNOW there is more, then write a dream or vision for your future below. It is alright if you do not know all of the details or if the picture is not yet perfectly clear. Write what you have today or schedule a time to come back and write it later.

_____

_____

_____

It's a choice, a decision to be made. What kind of life you desire is up to you. Don't deprive the world of your gifts and talents that are meant to be shared and experienced by others. Are you here to just take up space, or would you prefer to use your space to live the life you were created for and to help others along the way?

Wherever you are today, whether you don't believe you're even capable or deserving of dreaming, or you have begun to feel the tugging but have no idea what it means, or your heart is on fire and you can't seem to match the action to your desire, let these pages guide you towards the door that is waiting to be opened. We hope the words we so carefully chose offer you encouragement and inspiration to fill your soul with the craving and longing to dare to dream, dare to cast a vision for your life, dare to chase after your goals and the things that matter most to you!

Dig Deeper!

To uncover means to become aware of something you did not know. For some of us, the thought of uncovering parts of ourselves we are not already aware of is frightening. As if the things we already know aren't enough of a caseload to deal with. So we avoid the effort required and keep it stuffed deep down where we will never have to confront it. Can you imagine if nobody was brave enough to confront the primary need for warmth by creating fire? And what about the epiphany of sliced bread? These findings all started from distant dreams. Something we were once not aware of, but thankfully these things were unveiled so many could benefit from one person's dream.

Digging deeper ultimately leads to becoming a better version of yourself. It takes time, energy, and commitment to flush out a dream, work on our old mindsets, and build new habits. And this is where many of us get discouraged and retreat into an old stuck mindset. We want it to happen in a day, a week, or if we are feeling generous, we will give it an entire month. When the gap between here and there doesn't automatically close or significantly narrow, we are tempted to give up. Here's the thing: becoming a better version of yourself is a continual process. There will always be a better version, and you will always have the choice to evolve. You can always dig deeper.

Now you are getting in the right lane for your future, where the moving forward synergy of life starts coming together, and your outlook on life begins to reshape itself.

We said YES to this dream, this calling we knew God put in us a long time ago to actively pursue and bring to real life. You have already taken a small step of faith towards believing there is more for you, and guess what: THERE IS!

Get curious, get excited, BE BRAVE and have courage. Prepare your heart to say "YES" and OPEN the door to fulfill that calling on your life. Your calling is wrapped up in your purpose. Your impact on the world, your fulfillment of life will first come as a dream, a wish, a hope to be released. If you want to walk on water, the first thing you have to do is get out of the boat!

We not only want to prime the pump for your dreams to develop, but it is also time to put hands and feet to work and make these dreams a reality. We are here as your guide to walk you through a few steps that will help you move forward and take meaningful action. Without fulfillment, a dream is just a good idea that you wish had come to pass. The power of your dream is that it is meant to be fulfilled, brought to life in all of its fullness and power, and experienced by others.

You are **HERE**
wondering what your dream is.

You are **HERE**
where your imagination is being ignited.

You are **HERE**
excited about what you'll
discover along the way.

You are **HERE**
being brave.

WHY A
WHY?

chapter six

What's Driving YOU?

➡️ You were created by the Creator to create.

➡️ Everyone has a dream to be fulfilled and a message to be shared.

➡️ And knowing your Why, your truth behind your dreams, is what will get you there.

Definition of why (wī, hwī) -adv.
For what purpose, reason, or cause; with what intention, justification, or motive.
conj.
1. The reason, cause, or purpose for which
n. pl. ***whys***
1. The cause or intention underlying a given action or situation

2. A difficult problem or question.

Why Do You Need a Why?

Knowing the reason for your dream will bring purpose to the forefront of who you are and what you were created to do over your time here on this Earth. A *Why* is the foundational belief in what you do and what drives you to do it. You must be able to define why you want to achieve your dream. Your *Why* is what will determine how you get out of bed in the morning. It will serve as your compass and clear the path for energy or passion to ignite inside of you. Once ignited, you can see more clearly, decide more confidently, and stay engaged in activities when the terrain gets bumpy.

Let's apply this "you need a why" concept to your everyday behaviors.

➡ Why did you get out of bed today?

➡ Why did you make an appointment or schedule that meeting?

➡ Why did you pick up your kids from school?

There are reasons we do the things we do. Take the time to reflect on your *Why* so you can tap into the power it holds. There are either positive or negative consequences produced by your choices and behavior. What you will learn in this chapter is that your purpose, your reason, your *Why*, are critically important. This can be the key to putting your life in drive and getting out of that stuck place you have been in for so long.

What do you focus on? When you decide to focus on becoming a better you, you must give it meaning; and it must have value to you. That meaning becomes your *Why* for where you are going daily— knowing your *Why* and anchoring to it is what produces the emotion that fuels your passion. Once the emotion is ignited, action will have no choice but to follow! It is the constant igniting of that emotion that creates energy to propel you in the direction of an invisible goal that you are trying to make visible.

> The two most important days in
> your life are the day you are born and
> the day you find out why.
>
> MARK TWAIN

What You Focus On Will Grow

If you want to grow your dream, you will need to attach a *Why*. Without it, your dream is left floating in the atmosphere, in jeopardy of being swept away. The *Why* is what you turn to when the going gets tough. It is what you pull out of your pocket when you are exhausted, deflated, and up to your knickers in mundane details that no one warned you were going to be a part of your glamour-packed dream. Your *Why* will provide an endless supply of "go get it," "bring it on," "ha-ha you thought you could take me out today but you can't" attitude.

Responding to the *Whys* in our lives is the fuel for our future. It's the driving motivation to create, to fulfill, to have success, and to pursue our passion and purpose.

With a larger-than-life *Why* guiding you, you'll be more inclined to keep your eye on the prize because your *Why* is bigger than any excuse, obstacle, or obnoxious roadblock that will unquestionably find its way into your lane. Against the backdrop of your *Why*, all problems or setbacks are solutions waiting to be found.

- It will supply you with new and lasting energy. A Why stems from a core belief that you are already passionate about—it runs through your spirit and offers an endless source of strength to draw from.

- It will bring deeper meaning into your life. It will help you rearrange your priorities and focus on what really matters.

- It creates an overarching theme where all ideas, decisions, thoughts, and actions filter through and begin to align. Your life will begin to flow in a unified direction towards your goals.

- You will stay true to yourself as you stretch and develop your growth areas.

- When you commit to living your life with a purpose, doors open for amazing things to happen.

We all want to wake up every day with a sense of mission and purpose and align our actions with what we believe we were put on this Earth to do. But, what if something is blocking you from unlocking the *Why* that will get you there. Many different reasons are causing our struggle to unleash our *Whys*. When our *Why* gets lost, our mission and vision struggle. Here are some hurdles to be on the lookout for.

Your Why Is Nowhere to Be Seen

This is often a huge issue for people for one of two reasons; either you never discovered a real *Why* for your life or you lost it somewhere along the way. Sometimes we can choose the wrong *Why* by accepting the first idea that comes to us that sounds really good, YET that may not be our core *Why*. We all have to find our core reason for doing, our foundational purpose for being, and our primary motivation for moving forward.

Unfortunately, we make thousands of decisions and turns every day without putting much emphasis on why we chose that direction. Sometimes we just do it because it's expected, it's already been set in motion, or because it's part of our already ingrained routine. There's not much consideration or thought process behind it. Our decisions are happening TO us instead of intentionally creating a life that is FOR us. Honestly, if you don't know why you do something, how can you truly know what you are doing? If we don't understand the reason behind our mission, then we will not be able to find success in it. We can tell when the *Why* is nowhere to be seen. Goals with no *Why* are typically full of complaints and frustration and usually fall apart before you have a chance to close in on the finish line.

You may be so caught up in your busy or routine life that you forget to pull over every so often to ask yourself if this is the life you actually want to be creating. Are these the things you want to be pursuing? Is your *Why* "bigger than yourself?" We can look for reasons to live and grow that are only for ourselves and only from ourselves, but that too will short-change the deeper reasons we strive for greatness. There has to be a purpose or a WHY; otherwise, we will wander without direction, unable to lock in on the desired target.

Whose Why Is It, Anyway?

➡️ Your *Why* can not be attached to someone else's dream for you.

➡️ It has to be the *Why* that aligns with your dream, your purpose, and your heart.

Oftentimes we walk through life attached to an identity that someone else envisioned and prepared for us. We didn't have the chance or never took the time to consider if that was what we really wanted. So, we assume an identity that was placed upon us and talk ourselves into accepting these conditions. There are many loving and even well-meaning people who can share or project dreams onto us. In the worst situations, they may be trying to control our dreams and our *Whys* because they are threatened by our potential and need to feel a sense of power over us. On the other end, there are also kind and caring family members who may have hopes and dreams for us. They might hope we attend a certain school, go into a certain trade or profession, countdown the days until we make them a grandparent, and so on. Truthfully, those projections from other people, well-intended or not, can consume our own dreams and dominate our *Whys*.

Another way we lose our *Why* is by outsourcing our work to someone else. It takes honest reflection and hard work to make these growth steps and identify our *Whys*. If we aren't sure what to do next, we may be tempted to copy someone else. We may hear someone else's *Why*, and it sounds good and looks good, so we assume it as our own. Well, that doesn't work either! You were not made to be a copy of someone else. There is only one of you, and you are a limited edition of the highest value! You might love what someone else is doing and want to partner with them; that is great. But still, at the end of the day, you have to have your own *Why*.

Establishing your *Why* and communicating your hopes and dreams can be scary. You may believe that other people's livelihoods or approval depend on you consistently being who you already showed them you were. If your mind is set on fear, you may worry that the expectations of someone else will never allow you to pursue what you really want. You may worry that suddenly coming home as a changed and renewed person may cause confusion and throw your family off. Plus, even if you were brave enough to tread against the grain and explore this new identity, one more aligned with your authentic self, you would have to give up prioritizing your old one. The one you are familiar with and the one you might assume everyone counts on. But that old identity is also one you know how to manage; it's safe and familiar for you. Do not allow your dreams, identity, and your *Why* to be anyone else's other than your own. We do not need to love well and live well because others need us to; we can love well and live well because we want to—see the difference? Everything is better and richer when our *Why* is safely and securely our own.

You Deserve It

Our old limiting beliefs work against us whenever a situation brings our value into question. They get in the way and restrict access to the life that exists for you. Some of you are skeptical of your worthiness for a *Why*. You may have already accepted the terms of your life and never dared to investigate any further. You believe that it is for other people—more capable people, more deserving people—who haven't already forfeited their chance. You may be thinking your life is as good as it is going to get, and who are you to be ungrateful by asking for more. And some of us are so convinced that our distorted views cause us to miss anything good that may be coming our way.

Have you ever felt like you did not deserve your own dreams, and *Why*? Why do you or did you feel that way?

_____

_____

_____

You are HERE, needing to believe that you deserve it. Cast out the lies and allow your own *Why* to enter the picture. This calls for a mindset shift to "why not me?" Open your heart to second chances. This is your opportunity to discover why you get up in the morning. This is where you grow and live life on purpose.

Finding The One

This is the place where inspiration and excitement collide. The pieces are starting to fall into place. Through these action steps and reflections, you can begin to build momentum to carry you forward. The problem is, not one of us on planet earth can sustain that energy or momentum forever. One day, one step, is not enough to carry us all the way to the finish line. At the first sign of resistance, opposition, or even just an off kind of day, we might abandon ship. It's easy to forget about the meaning and purpose of our actions when they are superficial. You must DIG deep to discover your *Why*; it will allow you to have a strong foundation and withstand the test of time. Identifying your *Why* and understanding how you are motivated unleashes an incredible power that will illuminate your path forward.

Hopefully, right now you are starting to wonder about what your *Why* is. And this can't just be any old *Why*.

The *Why* we have to figure out is the ONE, the main one, the one that taps into the true essence of who you are and why you were created to be here.

Finding the *Why* is crucial because it's about your life and doing what you value. It may be something you hadn't given much consideration to, or you stayed up all night dreaming about it for hours. When you find it, you will know because you will **feel it**. There is an energy to it, and something will **light up** for you in your body and your mind and spirit. In the movie ET, his chest would light up when he started to get close to "home," his love, where he belonged; and you will begin to feel that too. When your internal light starts to rev up, it will bring energy, hope, and focus. If your current *Why* doesn't cause fireworks, or cause you to sprint around the house or want to part the Red Sea, then keep digging.

Here are a few exercises to help you get closer.

Circle the words that resonate in you about WHY a *WHY* is important for you!!!

Guide	North Star
Compass	Anchor
Purpose	Destiny
Stability	Your Inspiration
Growth	Intrinsic Motivation
Pulls You Through	Your Reminder
Gives You Hope	Fuels Your Decisions
Life Force	Calling
Focus	Ray of Light in a Dark Place

Having a *Why* lights up your MOTIVATION and energy!

Have you ever been motivated by doing something you have no value in? Probably not. Most people will not waste time doing something that has absolutely no value to them. Take a look back at the words and phrases that you circled. Wouldn't you rather live with that motivation and energy?

Do not overthink these questions. Answer honestly and quickly!

I am inspired by…

_____

_____

I am motivated to do more when…

_____

_____

When facing a challenge, what motivates me to figure it out?

_____

_____

When something needs to get done, what gives me the energy to get it done?

_____

_____

What makes me think and dream beyond my own life and my own circumstances?

_____

_____

What makes me dream again?

_____

_____

What makes me feel hopeful?

_____

_____

Write out a goal and the reason behind it. My goal is to:

_____

_____

Because:

_____

_____

Let's find out more about you and what drives your thoughts and actions. All of us are motivated in different ways. Once again, self-awareness is key. You have to know what motivates you as it is imperative to the success of your goal. If we are waiting to feel like doing something, it may never happen. Knowing yourself and how you thrive and grow will create the forward motion you need to get there.

Know Thyself

Discovering your *Why* is undoubtedly an essential part of this journey. For you to cross the finish line, it has to be paired with a healthy sense of awareness of who you are. Many people have a clear *Why*, yet their emotional intelligence about who they are isn't either clear or accurate.

"Emotional Intelligence" is defined by Daniel Goleman as "knowing one's internal states, preferences, resources, and intuitions." As you develop a stronger sense of awareness of who you are, your thinking will open up. With an open mindset, it becomes easier for you to make the necessary changes in your thoughts and perceptions, which will ultimately change your behavior.

Self-awareness causes intentionality in our thoughts, emotions, and actions. Once you tap into a more accurate view of who you are and move towards it, your self-awareness will increase your vision for your new life. You will begin to notice things about yourself that will either move you towards your goals or bog you down. Once you align your heightened and healthy sense of who you want to become with your *Why*, look out! Progress and traction will take place!

What Force is Driving You

When we are young, we intrinsically have big hopes, big dreams, and we-can-do-it attitudes. Then life rolls out and sometimes rolls over all of that. We are here to share a life-changing message with you. It's still there, inside of you, no matter what has "rolled over you."

Life motivation comes from the deep longings of the heart and the passion to see them fulfilled urges you on.

PROVERBS 16:26 (TPT)

We all have an inner voice within us; it was placed in us since our inception. This inner voice is a voice of love and wants us to do great things in our lives. It is a divine spiritual voice that wants to see us succeed and fulfill the divine message and dream placed within each of us. My inner divine voice is from the one who I know put a dream and a message in my heart, specifically for me, only to be fulfilled by ME. It's the voice that gave me hope a long time ago to believe for more. So, where does your hope and motivation come from?

Motivation is what drives us to get up and pursue things in life that have meaning to us—our dreams, goals, fulfilling our passion, our calling, our lifestyle desires. Knowing what motivates us can help when things don't go as planned or get difficult. One of our core motivations for writing this book is to help you figure out who you are and how you are wired so that you can cross the finish line of your goals and dreams! Motivation is like your accelerator. It creates perseverance to propel you through!

Intrinsic Motivation:

I have known for most of my life that I am an intrinsically motivated creature. Long before I understood this was how God intended to wire me, I used to think I was one strange cat. Even die-hard cat lovers have to admit, cats are kind of strange animals. God must have found it amusing to wire me this way! I read for fun, I enjoyed engaging in things that were challenging for the sake of the challenge, and I gained immense personal satisfaction when I became the first person in my family to graduate from college while simultaneously dreading the thought of having to participate in any sort of graduation ceremony. I do not require medals, awards, or special accolades to feel satisfied with my accomplishments. In fact, I would do anything to ensure this attention wasn't directed my way. The goals I set out to pursue come from a place deep within, and I take pure delight in knowing that my need for autonomy, competence, and connection have been quenched. Learning a new language is on my "things to do in my lifetime" list and not because I have a trip to some foreign land planned, although it will come in handy if I ever do. I exercise to push my personal limits to new margins. I clean because I like everything nice and tidy, and if I'm brutally honest, also because I have a slight case of OCD.

We are all wired differently, and that includes what motivates us and our view of what a reward should look and feel like. If you are like me, you are more intrinsically motivated by a task. We enjoy completing a task simply for the sake of doing it; our reward is the satisfaction of enjoying the activity. Another person can accomplish the same activity with an extrinsic motivation style. It is important to note that both versions can be effective.

Extrinsic Motivation:

This was a game-changer for me. For a long time, I viewed myself as lacking motivation or being lazy. I was envious of others who were more disciplined and pursued habits that propelled them to achieve great goals and success. And yes, discipline and good habits are essential too. Yet for me, my motivation for pursuing habits did not always line up with what good discipline would require. THEN, one day, I had a big AHA moment. I learned, with my open growth mindset, that people can be intrinsically or extrinsically driven in very different ways because of how they are wired. I discovered that I was more motivated by external payoffs, or extrinsic motivations. This was an immediate turning point! Extrinsically motivated people value external benefits such as positive outcomes, making money, raises, deadlines, perks. Additionally, they can also become highly motivated to achieve in order to avoid negative consequences.

You may find, as I did, that as you journey forward, your motivational values can shift, and what may not have had importance to you before now has more value.

Think of a time in your life when you felt a passion or positive energy about what you were doing? You felt aligned with your purpose, gifts, and talents. What were you doing? What sacrifices did you make to get to it? Are you a service-driven job type of person or skill or task-driven job type?

If money wasn't an issue, whom would you help, and how? Or how would you like to make an impact in this world?

My current motivational style is:

_____

_____

I am best motivated by:

_____

_____

Where do you want to be in 1 year, what would you be doing, and how would you act?

_____

_____

Dreams without Goals Are Just Dreams. Goals without a Why Are Empty Suggestions.

Knowing your *Why* is equally as important as having a dream and deciding your goals. Just as an engine is made up of multiple components, each serving its specific function, so is your dream. One without the other will most definitely deliver unsuccessful efforts. Self-awareness is all about understanding why you do what you do and is essential to guide your direction. Knowing your *Why* begins to fuel your actions and moves you forward.

The moment you truly start to lock in on your truest, most authentic, most powerful, what-you-were-created-to-do *Why* you will know it! You will feel a pure wave of attunement, and everything in you responds to it, aligns with it, and screams YES to it. All the red stop signals begin to turn green, the checkered flag goes down, and the race begins. SUDDENLY you know you found it! It may have taken a while to get there. For many, there were years and years of enduring hard terrain.

Hopefully, your perceptions have begun to shift about yourself, and the passion of your *Why* has started to bubble up with a fresh burst of energy and hope. Once this synergy starts to take place, you will feel it, love it, taste it, and want to run towards it. Take it in and remind yourself that you WERE made for more. Hold onto your open mindset and seek personal growth as your dream will need it to come to fruition.

Big dreams and goals are based on completing small incremental steps, step by step, "brick by brick to make it stick." The next chapter is about stepping into your dream and building a plan for it. Most of us can accomplish small things independently of each other, but when it comes to bigger goals and dreams, we fall short because they require more attention, more effort, more perseverance, and a much longer stretch of road to get there. Yet this long winding road is where **BIG**, extraordinary life-fulfilling things begin to develop. Did you know that when you add up all the small, seemingly mundane accomplishments and mix in a little bit of *Why* they begin to take on a new purpose and new meaning?

For some of you, this is your beginning. YOU ARE HERE, believing there just might be something to this for you. You have pushed back all those old limiting beliefs and discouragement from the past and opened up a new door in your life. Open that door, let the light shine in on you. Believe that you were made for more, and look deep within—that's where the treasure is. This is where you will find what you were created to create to change your life and impact your world!

You are **HERE**
SAYING I AM READY!

You are **HERE**
to seek and find your purpose.

You are **HERE**
believing it can happen.

You are **HERE**
ready to GO FOR IT!

STEPPING
INTO IT

chapter seven

Y ou have made it this far! It has been a long journey
already, and we still have a way to go. Kudos to you
for showing up. This work is not for the faint of heart. It takes
dedication, determination, and a strong desire to want to live a life
full of purpose. The internal effort you have made to clear some
space for your dreams to grow has been no small feat. You've had
to take a hard look at where you are, how you got there, and begin
to say "yes" to things that may have looked intimidating from your
current vantage point. You have started to understand some of the
conditions that have caused you to be rerouted from your God-given
plan. You have dug yourself out from the muddy traps you may have
been stuck in for far too many years. You have taken inventory and
uncovered the external and internal forces that are working against
you. This is the golden nugget, the place you will want to revisit
often. I know it's not fancy or luxurious, and there's definitely not a
spa where you can sit back and relax, but it provides a longer-lasting
richness that will not fade the moment you return home and begin
unpacking your bags. It is not one and done, I'm good, fully restored,
never looking back kind of work. These challenges will resurface,
especially when pressed up against new territory. Especially when you
are chasing the God-intended plan designed specifically for you. Put
it in the to-be-expected column and plan to return to the previous
chapters as many times as it takes to keep your head above the fray
and from returning to old, familiar, no-longer-serving-a-purpose
routes.

The mind that opens
to a new idea never returns to
its original size.

ALBERT EINSTEIN

Gradually we began veering off into uncharted territory and priming the pump for you to dream and expand the possibilities you may or may not have had any idea even existed. Your soul is being stirred; hopefully, you are beginning to peek beyond the doors in front of you. This is where the rubber meets the road, and a full-blown commitment is required. Buckle up; it's ALL IN from here! Once you have dedicated yourself to a life of dreaming and pursuing greatness, it's time to inscribe your Why, the deeper meaning that will provide rocket fuel for your dreams. Carve it in a piece of wood, engrave it on a plaque you can hang above your nightstand, tattoo it on your forearm where it's within your line of vision every single day. Your Why is the driving force to yield the best results for the greatest chance of success.

He who has a WHY to live
for can bear almost any how.

FRIEDRICH NIETZSCHE

If you are new to the world of dreaming and unlocking the desires of your heart, this section is going to offer a set of guidelines to help you identify what your dream is, what to expect as you begin to pursue it, and how to chase after it. We are going to ask you to go for a little more than your usual vanilla, and dive into a giant bowl of Gimme S'more. Think back to when you were a child and believed everything was possible. There is nothing off the table today. Any idea, no matter how big or small, is brilliant and worthy of your attention if it produces a burning deep down in your soul. Begin seeing yourself open to every idea that finds its way in. Embrace any new or different possibilities or interests that you may not have noticed before.

Remember, to start, you do not need to have the full itinerary mapped out. The path ahead can be 1,000 miles wide or 10 inches narrow. As long as you have a vision in mind, you will find your way. If you want to follow your dream but you are sitting here feeling blank and staring out in space, hoping one drops from the sky, there is only one place to begin: Step into your new lane of **discovery**.

A Sense Of Wonder

Notice the tugging on your heart. If you feel a constant attraction towards something, you are on your way to uncovering your dream. Begin paying attention to things you already love to do. Do you feel a sense of new life rush in when you help someone organize a closet? When you see the advertisement for the next 5K pop up on your feed, do you feel a stirring in your soul to almost click the register button? Write down a note about the last time you saw something or did something that made you wonder… "What if?"

_____

_____

_____

Allow your mind to wander, unrestricted, unimpeded, and free from limits. What are some things that you really care about? How do you enjoy spending your time? Close your eyes and let your mind (without doubt or skepticism) drift into the "if you could do anything dream-land." Begin to wonder about doing things in your life that would be great for you, your family, and the world. I know this is a risky move because you may not pick it back up, but set this book down and take 10 minutes to dream and jot down any thoughts that come to you, big or small, during this process. Don't discount anything! There are no right or wrong answers. All ideas will lead you to where you're going. Some are indicators to go a different way, some will be flashing caution lights, and some will illuminate the path going forward. Don't let these ideas fade away into the background. It's time to capture them. Get out a sheet of paper, a journal, a billion sticky notes, and start writing down any thoughts that surface. Anything that comes to mind, regardless of how silly or insignificant it seems, write it down without verifying the possibility of it or if it's crazy thinking! There's no time like NOW to take time and be present for yourself.

Discover Themes & Patterns

At this point, you may have a growing belief and resolve that there is more out there for you, but not many specifics of what "more" entails. That's okay. Today is the day that you will begin to uncover the common themes of your life that will help you focus your attention and energy on the right spaces. A great place to start is to pay attention to the activities, movies, books, and sources you are most attracted to. When you interact with others, what do you value most? When you are having fun, what are you often doing? If you've got to plan a trip, where would you go? When you get to pick a movie or show, what do you gravitate towards? Carve out a time each day for the next week and be mindful of the consistent themes and patterns that keep resurfacing. Unless you have the memory of a Tempurpedic foam mattress or you've memorized the first hundred digits of Pi, you will be best served taking notes with great detail.

Take in those moments of joy and inspiration, what you feel and when, why you felt that way and how you responded. Also, be mindful of the opportunities and activities that you do not enjoy. Identify what aspects of that moment were uninspiring or flavorless. With a little time and dedication, you will begin to find patterns and themes. You will be one step closer to understanding what inspires you, what you may want to steer clear of, and what type of interests bring meaningful energy into your life.

Again, the more honest and specific you get—the better. Applying an accurate description of your theme will allow you to develop a better, more intentional relationship with your daily life. This will help usher in a new enthusiasm for activities you once viewed as routine. It will give meaning and purpose to everything you do.

This is the dream we carry through the world
that something fantastic will happen
that it has to happen
that time will open by itself
that doors shall open by themselves
that the heart will find itself open
that mountain springs will jump up
that the dream will open by itself
that we one early morning
will slip into a harbor
that we have never known.
Olav Hauge

Here's what happens when you open up to discovering your dream. <u>You will</u>:

➡ Feel more alive.

➡ Grow curious about what's ahead.

➡ Ask more questions.

➡ Have hope and believe for more.

➡ Feel happier as you take a step closer.

➡ Crave more depth!

There is no straight line, perfect formula, or flawless method when exploring your dreams. It requires more of a trial and error approach. However, within all the testing and missteps comes a stirring, a kicking up of compacted dirt where your dream now has room to begin emerging. Each newly uncovered thought or idea will serve a purpose to put you in the best possible position to lock you in on your desired location.

Pay attention. Watch as your progress begins stacking upwards in the direction of your dreams. Start preparing yourself to say "hello" to your new vision by surveying the surrounding areas.

Broaden Your Horizons

Play on repeat, examine, reexamine, and embrace all new territories you are exposing. Each uncovering provides a fresh perspective to measure against, which will ultimately lead to expanded horizons. Read and study in areas of your greatest interest, which will give you new thoughts and expand things you haven't considered before. I had many interests that pulled me in so many different directions. I loved yoga, I wanted to help people, I cared deeply about social issues, I was intrigued by how to effectively tell a story. Just about every masterclass mentioned created a spark of curiosity in me. I listened to hundreds of TED talks on topics ranging from how to be an opportunity maker to why people believe weird things and everything in between. There was a period of time I opened myself up completely to learning about any topic that petitioned for my attention. As you broaden your horizons, you will strengthen your areas of interest. What doesn't serve you will drop off, and a sense of clarity will begin to form.

Take A Screenshot

Put up pictures of people and things that inspire you. Let's face it, we have so much competition for our attention these days that our memories have been reduced to the lifespan of a goldfish. This screenshot will serve as your daily visual reminder of what inspires you, what motivates you, what you are being drawn towards, and the big Why of what it's all about. Creating a vision board or whiteboard outline means you are serious about what you want your future life to look like. You are speaking it out loud. You will start to see it, feel it, and experience it as your steps are led by the vision you have placed in the forefront of your mind. Your mind will start to be attracted to this purpose. You will see it everywhere; even small mundane tasks will take on new meaning. Like you, your vision will evolve numerous times throughout this process, and you will keep building it as you go. The more you zoom in, the more clearly you start to see your dream, the more clearly you can see your purpose. My vision board today looks much different from the one I created two years ago. It has loftier goals. I've expanded my horizons and found new inspiration.

Refresh Your Network

Read about and try to meet people you admire and who inspire you. As you take in new ideas, you will feel energy, motivation, and the "watch what I can do" attitude will immediately outweigh any doubts or lies that made their way through the cracks. On the days you forget where you were headed, all it takes is one click of a YouTube play button to instantly reset the faith you have in your dream. One listen to Denzel Washington telling me to "Do what the 99% are not doing," I fall right back in my lane. Find people at your church, network in your community, join a group of like-minded dreamers who are on similar paths to engage with. When the atmosphere is filled with brand new, fresh, inspiring energy, it will pour over into you. And guess what, when you are full, you will begin pouring into those around you.

Well-Oiled Machine

Get your body in optimal shape to pursue your dream. There is a direct correlation between your energy level, motivation, and the performance of your body. Not only does working out give you more energy and a clear mental focus towards the tasks in front of you, but as you make it a priority in your life, other areas begin to take shape. This is not about having an athlete mentality and well-defined muscles. The state of your body is just as important as the state of your mind. When physical activity and absorbing healthy nutrition becomes a regular part of your life, you open the capacity to transfer motivation, habits, and discipline towards other things, like your dreams. Perhaps it happens by osmosis, or more likely, you begin to become more aware of the choices you are making. If you committed to working out in the morning, you would go to bed earlier. If you clear space in your day for meal prep, you will be less inclined to use that time to scarf down an entire six-pack of cupcakes. Tune up so you can tune in.

"YES" Is Your Catalyst

It's in the YES that your purpose begins to unfold. You are stretching yourself. I lived a better part of a decade, carrying around my potential, my dreams, my hopes and aspirations for an upgraded future in a separate backpack ready to be used only in case of emergency. I was aware enough to know this precious cargo was too good and important to put down, but every time I looked back and caught a glimpse of it out of the corner of my eye, I was reminded how tragic it seemed to be carrying around something of such great value knowing I may never get the chance to use it. I've known for a long time there was more ahead, and yet that wasn't enough to release the paralyzing grip of wanting to know the full outlay of the region ahead before I could commit to venturing into unknown territory. I like to have my ducks in a row, I like to make educated decisions, and I most certainly prefer to know what to expect ahead. It wasn't until my world was shaken, and I found myself in the middle of a state of emergency, that I realized what was in that bag was meant to be used.

I realized there's no point in carrying something all the way to the end, only to have it become dust and ashes by the time you get there. It was during that season I unzipped that bag and released all the "absolutely," "of course," "I'll do that," and "heck yes"— that is when I began stepping out of my own imagination and into something much bigger. It was in those first few steps where the floodgates opened, making room for new energy, new ideas, and new possibilities. At first, the steps were small, and to an outsider, may have seemed insignificant. However, I felt these steps with great intensity and intentionality. Every one of them mattered and contributed towards a greater goal. Were there moments I was uncomfortable, unsure, underqualified? Of course, lots of them. Trust me; I remember them vividly as my body was literally shaking all the way through each new "yes" and place of stretching. However,

I knew this discomfort was the price of entry into a meaningful life. Therefore, my desire for a higher purpose had to be greater than any awkward encounter I would have.

So, I kept stepping forward, one shaky leg at a time. The entire vision wasn't clear yet; I didn't know exactly where I would land, but my north star provided all the light I would need to press onward. I knew the direction, but the details were still vague. I took what I knew and began running with it. What I did know was I wanted to help people, so I said "yes" to leading a group. I knew mind, body, and spirit were a part of the story I wanted to tell, so I signed up and completed a 200-hour yoga teacher training. I knew in order to help people, I would need to have credibility and credentials, so I completed life-coach training. I listened, read, absorbed countless hours of material related to personal development, yoga, and sermons. As you begin stepping into your direction, theme, what inspires you—the details and opportunities will emerge. And as dreams would have it, the more you step, the more you feed them, the more you chase after them, the sooner you might catch them.

And that's exactly what happened. One day, the COVID pandemic abruptly arrived and drastically changed the landscape of our lives. This time was filled with uncertainty and a paring back of our lifestyles as each month went by. Then it happened—an unexpected opportunity opened up for me to co-author a book. I had a timeline for writing a book which had been a floating dream in that old backpack of mine labeled "for a later time," and yet it was very clear—almost instantaneously—that the Lord had called out that dream for such a time as this. Everything within me resonated, and I screamed, "YES, let's do this!" That dream became a reality at that very moment. It was the "YES" that gave actual hands and feet AND a destination to our dream.

Your Dream Needs A Whiteboard

Once your dream becomes something you absolutely, unequivocally believe can be true, it shapes your path forward through life and starts to shape you. Dreams bring us joy! Your dream needs a whiteboard, a space to exist and grow. The whiteboard and markers and erasers and post-its became symbols that something important was about to happen. When you put the dry erase marker in your hand and write your dream on the top of the whiteboard, your dream becomes an actual goal.

Take a moment to finish this sentence: My life would be so different and wonderful if...

_____

_____

_____

Writing our dreams on whiteboards and giant post-its paved the way for our book to take its first breath and come alive... **it becomes REAL**.

When you tell someone about it... **it becomes REAL**.

When you start your day and end your day thinking about what's next... **it becomes REAL.**

When you do things that make it **REAL**... your world will open up like never before.

As **it becomes REAL**, you will NOTICE so much more happening in your life from the inside out! Here are some things you will feel when you write out your dream.

- A new awareness, you will see it everywhere and your mind starts to search for it.

- Your energy and motivation increase.

- A relentless hunger to seek, learn and grow.

- Old fears and worries fade away, doubt declines, hope and confidence show up.

- Old habits aren't appealing anymore because you know there is more!

- Alignment with your authentic self and what you were created to do.

- Everything now seems possible!

There's a distinct route to turning your dream into real-life action. Below is a set of directions to get you there. Don't speed through this part of your journey, or you will miss some important key aspects and may have to u-turn and start over. Mapping out your route is unique to you, so don't let a Google search do it for you;

otherwise, you could also end up somewhere on a dead-end dirt road without a name that's not even on the map! John Maxwell teaches the value of developing a clear and compelling vision of your dream first, in order to set the goals that will get you there. Clarity will affirm your purpose, define an order to priorities and provide you with a map to get there. Here's where you can begin to outline what you want to accomplish.

1 - Pick one dream, the one change or event in your life that would make the most difference right now, and the one that can make the most significant difference for your future life. Single focus brings clarity and enhances your success in achieving what you want! Too often, we dream about all of our dreams and never get one off the ground.

2 - Pick one goal that will help you move closer to your dream. This is something that you can accomplish that will help make your dream a reality. It is almost like a mini dream on its own, but it is anchored with the same purpose and Why as your main dream.

3 - Map It Out: Whiteboard it, post it, vision board it. Establish mile markers to help you create a course or road map.

You will get to repeat those steps over and over again. As you identify and grow your dreams, your whiteboard and map will grow and develop as well. You will get better and better at charting the course to take you there. Hopefully, you have selected one dream for yourself at this point. We want to help you keep dreaming and prepare a vision for your future self by putting all of the pieces together.

Now is the time to pick one goal that will contribute to your dream and your *Why*. To build out your goals, we will use the *SMART* process. This means that your goals and action steps can be lined out in this order.

S ▶ Specific and detailed

M ▶ Measurable to see progress

A ▶ Achievable and realistic

R ▶ Relevant and connected to who you are

T ▶ Time-Bound

Here is a look at our process and example for picking the dream, goals, and mapping it all out.

Our Goal = To publish a book that communicates our message to help others.

Now, we branch out our action steps, or "mile markers," that will help us execute our goal and bring us closer to making our dream come true. Your action steps will fill the gap between where you are today and the goal that you've selected. Here is how we mapped out our goal with mile markers.

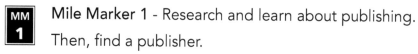 **Mile Marker 1** - Research and learn about publishing. Then, find a publisher.

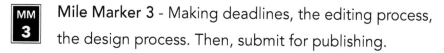 **Mile Marker 2**- Determine what our book is about, learn how to write, expand our knowledge base and talk to people who are doing what we want to do. Then, write the book manuscript.

 **Mile Marker 3** - Making deadlines, the editing process, the design process. Then, submit for publishing.

 **Mile Marker 4** - Research social media and marketing, talk with experts, develop our brand, establish a strategy. Then, launch our book! We made it!

Notice, each mile marker has clear action steps to take and a specific landmark achievement. We cannot move on to Mile Marker 2 without a publisher, and we cannot move on to Mile Marker 3 without a written manuscript. The last Mile Marker leads us to the destination of this goal. We have completed this audacious goal and have achieved something amazing along the way. Most importantly, we are closer to our dreams being a reality than we have ever been before. Now, we repeat the process and determine our next goal and begin to map it out on the whiteboard.

Remember to Surrender

Throughout this process, we have sought God's infinite wisdom and insights to be impressed upon all who read this book. Our hope and prayer is that you will be filled with great hope and know that your life can change. The GOOD NEWS is that we are all invited to change. You are invited to become your best self and to impact the world as only YOU were designed by God to do. For us, the divine intention is our guiding light, our courage to be brave and push through with our faith propelling us to make a difference to those around us. Each of us has a unique path to follow to reach our destination. It was truly a divine moment when we said "yes" to writing this book, and it became a huge pivot for what's ahead in our future.

Believing in a bigger-than-yourself God for your bigger-than-yourself dreams is a dynamic pairing. We were created to create and fulfill the dream that has been placed in each one of us. That master plan is based on all of your gifts, talents, and passions to be fulfilled only by you. All those continuous themes and tuggings over the years trying to get your attention was a divine plan to get you on track with your destination. Ultimately, a sure glimpse of God's plan for our lives should be all we need to hang on tight and enjoy the ride.

If you are reading this, then you may be the proud owner of a newly purchased whiteboard, hopefully with the first etchings of your future life. Look at it daily, think about it, pray about it, re-work it, and talk to others about it. It's a birthing process that belongs to only you and eventually will impact the world around you. You see, all of us have a dream for our lives inside of us; it's in our spiritual DNA. You have been hard-wired to fulfill it. There is a new story waiting to be told. The whiteboard is blank, waiting for you to begin writing out the version of you that fits who you truly are. It is time to capture all of the circling thoughts, floating daydreams, ruminating ideas and turn them into a reality—a reality that is free from discounting your abilities, convincing yourself you don't have what it takes, and reducing your perception of what's available to you. Those negative thoughts need to be crumpled up like a piece of paper and thrown in the trash where they belong.

You have a choice right now; the whiteboard is speaking. Dream Big! Begin preparing your mind, body, and spirit to receive the awesomeness you were created for. Cast your vision and attach tangible goals that push you towards this future version of yourself. Do not hesitate to start designing the life you envision. Begin walking confidently in the direction of your dreams. Or at least walk long enough to make it to the next chapter, where you can develop an appreciation of your abilities and talents. We know… it sounds like a lot? Breathe OUT any doubt and take IN a deep breath of assured CONFIDENCE.

You are **HERE**
searching for what will make
you feel fulfilled and valued.

You are **HERE**
opening your mind to unlimited possibilities.

You are **HERE**
believing there is a dream worth stepping into.

You are **HERE**
ready to take action!

CONFIDENCE MATTERS

Now that you are beginning to expand your beliefs of all that is available to you, it's time to focus your attention on the main event. You have traveled all this way, and we don't want your hard work and efforts to be futile because you are missing one particularly important ingredient. It would be like baking bread and forgetting to add the yeast!

When we first started researching for this chapter, which has had many titles, and the deeper we journeyed, the more obvious it became to us that our level of confidence is paramount to gaining traction towards our future. A few years ago, we began saying "yes." *Yes* to being open, *yes* to challenging our beliefs, *yes* to growing, *yes* to dreaming a big and scary dream. This led to a *yes* to leading a group, which by default meant *yes* to creating a curriculum. It was a *yes* to putting ourselves out there. I would like to imply it was a *"heck yes,"* but it was actually more like a white-knuckle grip on the familiar, "you better give me a push before I high-tail it out of here" type of *yes*. Today these all appear small and insignificant against the backdrop of an expanded vision. However, two years ago, they were huge and way out of the comfort zone for both of us.

A whole lot of *"yeses"* and gained insight later, we are deep in the trenches of unfamiliar territory writing our very first manuscript. What happened in between is the point we don't want you to miss. The yes to write this book came from a place of stacking a whole lot of other *"yeses"* on top of each other. Some were whispered with the hopes that no one else was close enough to hear, and some were met with a grand excitement difficult to contain. Through every one of these unlocked doors, there was still residual fear, doubt, and a slight sense of panic to keep in check. However, our willingness was reinforced with a new level of confidence that could only be gained through a thousand small steps into the great unknown.

This chapter was and still is the culmination of a beautiful discovery. It's about beginning to believe in the truest form of yourself, your authentic self, the one you were created to be. It is in this assurance where your dreams are given permission to unfold. As you trek through these chapters, our mission was for you to learn some essential things about yourself; things you need to say goodbye to and others that you should treasure, value, and keep tucked nicely in your back pocket to be accessed at a moment's notice. The latter are representations of your true self—the part of you that will want to SHOW UP and flourish in your life moving forward.

In the beginning, you were created perfectly. And yet, as we brush up against the world around us, we begin to redefine how we view ourselves—which seriously impacts our future efforts. It's absolutely possible to believe in who you were created to be, to have visualized your dreams for years, and yet never get them off the ground due to a lack of confidence. You can have all the knowledge and skills to run a successful business, be a rockstar parent, or open a yoga studio— and still lack the confidence to follow up with the concrete action required to fulfill these goals.

Earlier in the book, which probably seems like a thousand miles ago, we discussed self-esteem and how it comes from deep within. Self-esteem is how well you like yourself, what you think about yourself, are you a good person? I can tell myself all day that I am beautiful, I am loved, and I am _____. Heck, we encourage you to do exactly that. Start your day with a powerful "I am" statement and watch as you begin to transform how you view yourself. Do it every single day until you actually believe it. Do it until the overflow can no longer be restrained. Once you establish how you view yourself, you then have to decide just how sure you are of that judgment. This is CONFIDENCE—the belief that you can accomplish any task no matter the odds, difficulty, or adversity.

Confidence serves as a magnifier of our thoughts. When we magnify something, we are making it appear larger than it is. The bigger your "yes I can" attitude appears, the greater the belief that it's available to you regardless of any evidence that suggests otherwise. This is the pivotal point where our thoughts turn into actions! It is a necessary spark before everything follows. It is the difference between being inspired and getting started, between folding when the going gets tough and pressing in until it's done. Confidence invites us to operate with certainty. We show up differently when we know we can win versus when we hope we can win. The degree of your belief will determine the boldness of your action.

> Confidence is a belief in your ability to achieve success, which then stimulates action, you will create more confidence when you take action. It keeps accumulating, through hard work, through success, and even through failure. Sometimes we just have to stop thinking about it and just do it.

KAY KATTY & CLAIRE SHIPMAN

The Confidence Factor

Since the early 1900s, this has been the topic of a lot of research in the psychology world. The curiosity to discover why some people have more confidence than others, what factors affect it, and how to find the sweet spot where we have what it takes to get the job done has evolved and provided us with much-valued information to get ourselves to a new level of action!!

"Confidence comes from the Latin word 'fidere' which means 'to trust;' therefore, having **self-confidence** is having trust in oneself." Based on that definition, the assumption is that if you trust in yourself, your capabilities, knowledge, abilities, and experiences, then you would have a greater sense of certainty about what you will pursue.

Have you ever had to walk into a room full of people you didn't know? Can you remember how that encounter made you feel? Were you so concerned you may trip over your own feet that you forgot about the amazing blowout you just got today? Did you immediately map out the quickest route to the nearest corner hoping once you got there, it would activate the power of invisibility?

The more confident you are, the less influence the external world will have on you. The more you feel comfortable with yourself and do what you set out to do, the less the external things will control your life. If we don't follow through and prove to ourselves, we will be more susceptible to believing the lie. Here we are in **REAL TIME** in your life right now... let's do it.

Confidence is how we
meet our circumstances.

SHARON SALZBERG

Take a moment and read this statement three times.

Confidence is how I will meet my circumstances.

Confidence is how I will meet my circumstances.

Confidence is how I will meet my circumstances.

How are you meeting up with your circumstances today? Let's slow down and really think about how you have shown up and what your confidence level was at the time. Pick several situations from today or the past couple of days. One at a time, match that circumstance with the level of confidence you held around that circumstance.

"Confident"   "Nervous"

"Open To Try"   "Lacking Confidence"

"Bring It On"   "No Way"

"Maybe I Can"   "I Doubt It"

Confidence is what ultimately shapes your attitude and determines how YOU show up in your life. Sometimes there is a discrepancy between how we view ourselves and our capability to succeed. This gap is what causes us to put on the brakes and lowers our confidence. Building your confidence is the key ingredient for closing the gap. Confidence becomes the inertia that pushes us forward and presses down the old mindsets that are busy calculating the risk of you stepping out.

Sounds Easy Enough; Why Is It So Hard?

Far too many people are walking around every day without even a baseline level of confidence. A lack of confidence leaves our vocabulary filled with "can't," "won't," and "impossible." Compromised confidence drains us until all that remains are the remnants of our crushed dreams. Without confidence, we get stuck. When we are stuck, it is difficult to even get started. The biggest issue with a lack of confidence is that we won't get to the next level without it.

A general lack of confidence can occur based on how you were raised, including cultural and gender differences, negative environments, emotional internalizing, hesitancy, second-guessing, and lack of skill set for the task.

While looking back over the last few chapters, have you become aware of a theme or a cause for your low confidence in your efforts to move forward? Oftentimes our past can define our confidence in our present, holding us hostage to dream and reach for our best future life.

If you are not pursuing your goals and dreams, it will bother you. Feeling discouraged and defeated can deflate your confidence in your future. There will be an obvious tension due to the gap between where you are and where you want to be.

Are you waiting to feel competent to go after your dream? That may never happen because your view of your competency may be skewed! Looking back, it was a good thing that we didn't wait to write this book until we felt we had the competency to do it! What we had was a compelling inner sense that we were called to do it and a crazy confidence that we could learn how to do it and achieve it. We didn't base our decision on if we had accomplished it before, as this is where doubt can come in like a smashing wave. That type of perspective will keep you far away from stepping into your new must-be-more-to-life future. Pursuing a new skill or activity IS a learning experience… don't use that as a reason not to go after something you want. Flip your outlook about it.

Fear of Failure: How has this affected your confidence over the years? The fear of a bad outcome becomes your reference point for avoidance, which results in a lowered desire to pursue personal growth and follow your heart's desires. It becomes a self-perpetuating cycle of downplaying your potential. Fear wants to block our growth efforts! It has the power to impair the development of your "confidence muscles." Fear will minimize your confidence and dilute who you were destined to become.

When you lose sight or belief in yourself, you may notice some of the below behaviors:

➡️ Doubt and hesitation

➡️ Second guessing

➡️ Deters you from practicing, so you never get to feel or touch the energy of it

➡️ Blocks you from stepping into your dream

What's your worst-case scenario if you try and fail? There are endless stories of how many times people were rejected, failed, or were denied access to something they were in the pursuit of chasing. If it is a small dose of motivation you need, pick one—any one—of the world's most influential people and listen closely to their beginning testimonies. Every single one of them experienced some form of failure, yet they kept pressing on. Instead of retreating, they learned from it, developed new practices, and strengthened their resilience. Let's DEBUNK the fear of failure. Without at least trying to face your fears, you may live with regrets for the rest of your life. But there is a better option. Push through the thick cloud of fear to release its grip over your life and future. Do this and prove to yourself you can and open up endless opportunities to grow!!

Criticism: When someone critiques or speaks a negative assumption about you, does it bring your confidence into question? If so, it's because those words may pierce your heart with an arrow on what you currently perceive as a weakness or growth area. It exposes what we already believe about ourselves. We can easily start to slip back into some old self-doubting thoughts. Oftentimes, we take to heart the words of others so quickly without qualifying their motives. Guard your heart and mind and take in healthy feedback; this will move you towards a more positive focus.

Comparison Trap: Try to avoid this at all cost because it will cost you! You looked, and in seconds, you felt it… that spike of envy, that immediate flushing feeling over you that they have what you don't have or did what you didn't do. Oftentimes, nothing good comes from scrolling through social media, except instead of feeling energized, you are left feeling inadequate. Comparing yourself to others will affect your self-esteem directly, pulling you into that deep vortex of feeling inferior and bad about yourself. Your perspective is that you aren't doing as well as your friends or ALL the other random people on social media. If you continue to hit the thinking negative thoughts button, eventually, it will erode the positive energy of your confidence and allow that dark cloud of limiting beliefs to hang around, immobilizing you. It's truly a big energy zapper. Our greatest competition is not external. It is about ourselves and the internal battles we all face. It starts with you. This is a reality you can't escape; you have to deal with how you value yourself. When you begin viewing yourself in your future life, all the "others" will end up in your rearview mirror. Guard and protect the healthy self-image you have and keep it lined up with your vision.

Worry & Stress: Did you know anxiety, a.k.a worry on steroids, is a confidence crusher? The more hyperactive your brain becomes trying to eradicate the automatic negative thoughts (ANTS), the more overwhelmed and stressed you will feel. Research by Dr. Daniel Amen reveals that when your brain operates in an anxious state of mind, it can actually freeze up its ability to think creatively and spontaneously. Much of your brain's energy is focused continually on your state of anxiety and trying to manage it. As long as you allow your brain to keep spinning and ruminating, you can assure yourself of not operating to your full potential, which will ultimately affect your confidence level. It will be difficult for you to reach for your dreams.

Reconstructing Your Confidence

We have outlined some of the largest and more prominent enemies of confidence. Have you ever had a lack of confidence? Which of these areas have you struggled with the most? Be mindful of your confidence level as you move forward. Confidence can slip at any time. Maintaining confidence is not a static or stationary activity. We all need to reconstruct and build up confidence as we go!

Confidence Is A Skill: Would it surprise you to know that confidence is a skill that can be developed? Confidence is the ability to believe in yourself to accomplish any task no matter what difficulty or adversity you face. There's no magic button to push that will drop it from the sky when you need it. It's not either you're born with, or you're born without it. It happens by developing it, as with any other skill. The dilemma is you can't develop it unless the task or skill you are trying to accomplish is no longer new, and if you don't have the belief in yourself in the first place, how likely are you to try something new? So how do we get ourselves from amateur to wizard while building our self-confidence?

Anchor In: Know your truth. Know how valuable you are. Know your worth. If you don't know, you will accept what the world offers you. Don't ignore weaknesses and insecurities. Begin to build an understanding of where they may be coming from and constantly move in the direction to course correct and build your confidence. Nothing can penetrate your soul without your permission. Have a growth mindset. Start searching for opportunities to grow and learn instead of worrying about messing up. You will be surprised by the new energy you experience.

Leave Your Comfort Zone: The best way to build confidence is to step out, take a risk, and try new things. Anticipate and embrace the fail and view it as an opportunity to grow!! When you step out, no matter how small or big, you begin to practice things that will get you where you want to be. Growth leads to mastery and to a super-hero level confidence. When we first started this journey, we felt we were to say "yes" to new opportunities that came to us. Once we said that first "yes," the energy shifted, and we threw ourselves into a huge learning curve. We welcomed the firehose that was about to aim straight for our faces. We had the nerves and excitement felt when you get ready to take the plunge down a giant ski slope for the first time, but it has been so worth it. We never looked back! Don't sit back and let opportunity pass you by. You will regret staying in your comfort zone, yet you will grow confidence by leaving it.

Start Small: Stack your wins. Track all your accomplishments, big or small, and add them up at the end of a day. Accumulating gains increases confidence and motivates you to do more. This practice changed my life. Instead of letting the wins pass me by and drop off to the bottom of the ocean never to be seen again, I started capturing them. Write down your wins and victories. Bring them into your line of vision every single day. Did you cook something new for dinner… add that to your resume. Fix a plumbing issue without the help of a professional, sounds like a new skill to include in your repertoire. Did you add value to your workplace or family today? You are clearly on your way to rockstar status. As I began to group together all of these small wins, my confidence was exponentially compounded and shot up like bamboo.

Repetition: We expect to be confident but can't be until the task is no longer new to us. You have to do it a thousand times! The problem with repetition is most of us bail at the first sign of adversity. Why? Because our first line of defense is to draw assumptions and begin building a case that we are not skilled, talented, or clever enough to master something we've not yet encountered before. It is easier to accept defeat than it is to embrace initial failure. Practice, practice, practice, persistence, and then practice some more. My son has been playing soccer for the past ten years. He has shown up to hundreds of practices. He has dribbled the ball up and down the soccer field so many times I'm winded just thinking about it. He has repeated drills over and over until they are ingrained in his DNA. There have been games lost that were played with such a high level of technical skill and precise accuracy, and there have been games won out of sheer luck and pure grit. You can play well and lose; you can play poorly and win.

Confidence was present on both days because of the level of dedication put into practice.

Repetition is the driving force to building the muscle to gain mastery. Mastery is a product of lots of practice and hard work that creates and builds your confidence along the way. Those action steps require a "YES," no matter how big or small, relevant or irrelevant. Every step and every *yes* will begin to stack your confidence, elevating you to new heights as you spread your wings and begin to take flight.

> Practice creates confidence.
> Confidence empowers you.
>
> GYMNAST SIMONE BILES

Mastering just one thing will create new confidence to try other new and bigger things! The more you do, the more you stack, the more awesome your sense of confidence, the greater your belief to reach for the stars.

Self-Talk: What is your story? What is the narrative you repeat to yourself and others? Your story has a great influence on determining the path you will choose. How does your narrative affect your confidence? Are you paying attention to the good things you have done in your narrative, or are you still replaying your old narrative?

There are enough voices telling us we can't do it. Replace them with your own self-affirmations. I am_____ . Who else is going to tell you? Remind yourself daily of all the things that make you who you are. You are not defined by one single moment. Write a letter to yourself of all the things you are proud of and read it anytime doubt and fear begin to seep in. Stop the negative self-talk. Praise the positive behaviors you want to reinforce. Invite permission into your narrative. Permission for confidence to exist. Permission to defy expectations. Permission to chase after a life you can be proud of.

Accentuate Accountability: Accountability affirms and props up our confidence. It restores hope and builds certainty. It empowers you to keep going until you get there. Building a healthy community around you is the fuel to keep you in your lane, moving forward with the goals you are striving for. Surround yourself with people who are excited to watch you succeed! Their voices can speak wisdom, encouragement, love, acceptance, and whatever else you may need during those critical times.

Whenever we got low in energy or depleted of heart during the book writing process, we would reach out to authors or others in our circle for a breath of fresh air. These "atta girls" were delivered in just the right dose to keep us digging back in. Accountability creates energy. Know when you need it and seek it.

Command Your Confidence

Too often, a second of CLARITY will lead us towards a commitment to change; but because of old reflexes, we hesitate as new situations arise. Growing your confidence is the key to launching forward towards the passion you have for your dreams and goals. The degree of belief you have in yourself determines how you will present yourself to the world. Learn to face each day with enough confidence to press forward into unfamiliar territory and begin to watch your dreams unfold.

All of the chapters of this book have been leading up to this pinnacle point of a decision only you can make.

➡️ You have learned how and why your past has affected your present and future.

➡️ You have gained insight into who you were authentically created to be and maybe have an idea or two about how you want to take possession of your new future.

➡️ You have dared you to dream new dreams again.

➡️ You have dared you to dream new dreams again or to breathe life into the ones from long ago that still have a heartbeat.

Your *Why*, your purpose, your passion for life has become clearer than ever before, and you know you have to do something to stop the undertow of the familiar from pulling you back in. This is where we challenge you to stay on this adventure to a new and wide-open space of life waiting for you to continue to say "YES!"

Let's celebrate! YOU ARE HERE!

You are **HERE**
where permission to be
awesome is granted.

You are **HERE**
ready to claim what is yours.

You are **HERE**
where confidence overshadows fear.

You are **HERE**
where your dream is within your reach!

PART 3

LEVELING UP ⬆

PLAN FOR

SUCCESS

HONING YOUR HABITS

Far too many of us are getting up every morning with a solid level of enthusiasm, eager and ready to pour all our energy into the day in front of us, only to find ourselves falling FLAT by mid-afternoon. With our energy depleted, we are crawling on our knees by the end of a Monday afternoon. We have dreams, goals, and a *Why* to inspire and motivate us towards a greater purpose. But we just keep falling short. We can't seem to catch a break or gain enough momentum. We feel as if we have just lost another day in our quest to touch our dream. HERE and THERE begin to feel farther apart, and slowly we are less frequently trying to reach out for it.

Every single thought, choice, and action determines who you are becoming and which direction you are going based much on the habits of our lifestyles. Some are good ones, some bad, some old and no longer serving their original purpose. When you hit the snooze and skip the cycling class, it doesn't affect *only that* moment. Hal Elrod, the author of "Miracle Morning," summarized it best when he pointed out you are actually rewarding your brain and telling it that it is okay to do the old behavior instead of the new ones you said you wanted to do. There is a bigger picture. Every action matters. Every choice is developing your habit lifestyle.

We Are What We Repeatedly Do

When the glitz, glamour, and excitement of your dream wear off, habits are what will sustain you.

If we are doing nothing, that's our return to our life. It's scary to say, but have you ever driven to work and then don't remember driving there? Yep, that's your brain on autopilot. You have driven to the same location for years, your brain knows the way, and you are thinking about other things. It's become as automatic as your daily ritual of eating ice cream every night right before bedtime.

A habit is any action or sequence of actions initiated by a cue or a trigger. A cue could be a particular situation, conversation, event, person, emotional state, time of day, or even a location. The cue of a habit is what causes your behavioral response or your next action. Behavior modification is all based on the premise that if we get rewarded by a certain behavior, our brain, which houses our pleasure center, quickly learns it is good and will want to do it more often. Continued repetition of those actions eventually will happen without you thinking about it, and a "habit loop" is born! Eventually, your habits become as automatic as walking or scratching your nose. This is reflected in our biology. When habits are being created, there is activity in the decision-making areas of your brain—the prefrontal cortex and the hippocampus. Over time, as the behavior is repeated, the activation in the brain shifts to the same part of the brain responsible for moving your limbs. You're no longer thinking actively. Instead, you're responding with as much thought as it takes to move your arms or legs.

This is why changing habits can be challenging. You need a lot of repetition to replace an old habit with a new one. Your body will want to do what feels most routine and rewarding. So building consistency and focusing on the right rewards are important. A habit basically breaks down into four parts.

1. **Cue or Trigger** - This is what signals action to your mind and body; it calls for a response. Let's use the example of waking up on time in the morning. To set a cue for yourself, you use the alarm function on your phone or clock. When it's time, the alarm goes off, and the habit has been triggered for action.

2. **Routine** - This is your mental, physical and emotional response to the cue. Many of us have built up a poor habit in this arena, so our routine in this scenario may be to hit the "snooze" button. Our desired outcome is lost; our cue to wake up on purpose and on time has been denied as we drift back to sleep. Now, let's FLIP this habit into a stronger and more beneficial mode. The alarm goes off, and our new routine is to actually get up out of bed with purpose and reason. We had a plan, mapped it out, and we are going to seize the day and make every opportunity count!

3. **Reward** - You reap what you sow. For a short-term moment, hitting the snooze button provides an instant reward of more sleep. In this scenario, sleep is good, and it is something that we want. Wanting to sleep in is not a terrible thing. It is a healthy and natural function that we all need. However, while our poor habit rewards us with a little more sleep, it robs us of much more. Like other scenarios, the old habit is not helpful or healthy for us. The extra bit of sleep we get when

hitting the snooze button has been shown to be unproductive, and many believe it actually slows your mind and body down for the rest of the day. Poor habits bear shallow and often false rewards. On the other hand, if we awaken with our alarm and routinely get out of bed on time, our reward is the time and energy that we have earned and the satisfaction of achieving the goal that we set for ourselves. In this case, we have set our whole day up for success!

4. **Craving** - This is our habit loop. The rewards that our habits supply become what our body craves. If we constantly hit snooze, then our body will crave an unsatisfying and unhelpful reward of a few more minutes of unproductive sleep. If we awaken with purpose, our body will crave the energy and momentum of our healthy habit. Again, this is why breaking old habits can be difficult. Our body is craving something and will want what it is used to getting… until we train it to want something better.

Habits Are Powerful

The right habits can change the course of your life! Once you train your brain to build healthy daily habits, they will become as automatic as those OLD HABITS used to be. Seek and cultivate habits that are good for you, the ones that lead you to your purpose and dreams.

Here's some truth for you: your entire existence is one of great worthiness. You are just as qualified, capable, and talented as those around you who appear to be closing in on their dreams. You have come too far, worked too hard, and persevered for far too long to pull over and give up on the beautiful life you deserve. It is time for you to rise to the occasion. The foundation has been set, the dream has been identified, and the goals have been outlined. There is one thing separating you from achieving the goals that will lead you to the life you desire... and that is your *Habits*.

Imagine yourself waking up with the same amount of motivation and determination as someone who is purposefully chasing down their dreams. They appear to be effortless in tackling the challenges of their days. Everything they touch turns to success. People hang on every word they speak as if it should be chiseled on the marble floors in the museum of epiphanies. They don't seem to get frazzled or distressed when the wind picks up and blows the roof off. You see, we all have a certain amount of energy and willpower when we wake up each day, and we all get to decide how we are going to use it. To achieve our dreams, we must have a morning routine and daily habits that align with our values and priorities. These habits are what sets the stage for our entire day to aim at our target.

Habits have the ability to work for you or against you. Most of the time, we don't realize what our bad habits of sleeping in, skipping exercise, or eating unhealthy costs us. Without our awareness, our tank's reserves are being depleted. We fully understand the struggle is real. It has taken hundreds of failed attempts to break these old habits. But there is good news… each failed attempt was another shot, another chance to do something different. If we didn't fail, we would not have had the opportunity to step in the right direction. Developing and incorporating healthy, goal-guided habits is a major necessity if you have a dream to bring to fruition. The goal itself will never be enough to get you there. It is the healthy habits you form and follow along the way that set the foundation to build your dream.

We must change old patterns and embrace self-discipline and healthy habits. The results are worth it!

Turn Off the Autopilot

We have been working on habits and the morning routine concept for the better part of two years. Although we 100% believe in all the science and success stories resulting from highly effective habits, there have been some setbacks along the way. Even with our own levels of growth and experiencing first-hand knowledge of the benefits, there were lapses. Too much planned, not enough stuck, and so many resets back to the starting line. In fact, today, as we are writing this, we are starting a newer and improved version of both of our morning routine habits. However, there is also another opposing force working against our new efforts and yours. This force is the mysteriously unseen wielding the power of automation. And we don't realize its strength until it has rerouted our best laid out plan.

It is the daily ingrained coding of our automatic old habits lodged in a part of our brain called the *basal ganglia*. Statistics claim that 40-50% of our day is shaped by these automatic habits. Your brain has mapped in programming that you are going to hit the snooze button, talk yourself out of exercising, and take a hard-pass on getting up at your new time. Even the habits of responding to distractions such as rambling thoughts, device alerts, or emails have you on autopilot where you don't even decide, it just happens! Those "automated" habits aren't serving you well anymore and have to be replaced with new ones that advance your agenda! Again, you are literally battling against your old programming. Overcoming your autopilot takes extreme dedication and hard work.

Old Habits Die Hard

Your attempts at establishing new habits will definitely be challenged as you push for a breakthrough, so you need to have a strong *Why* to remind yourself of the reason you are getting up so early in the morning. You may have to be willing to give up things that are familiar or you've grown accustomed to. Even as you are reading this, you may be feeling some discomfort just thinking about getting up early. Prepare yourself for some big pushbacks to your brain's desire for instant gratification as you choose differently to pursue that long-term goal.

You aren't going to be happy when that alarm goes off at the crack of dawn or the cold shower to wake up, going out for that morning run you don't care for, eating healthy, praying more, reading, or planning out your day. BUT, we can promise you at some point, after pursuing it and being steadfast with what YOU say you want to achieve, you will eventually want to do it more. Well, maybe not the cold shower part.

Don't Quit

There are a lot of reasons people quit. First of all, quitting is really easy! Oftentimes when starting a new habit, especially one that may not be super fun at first, we quit for reasons we could have avoided or been better prepared for.

Here are four reasons WHY we quit before ever having a chance to appreciate the benefits waiting on the other side:

1. We don't see the results quickly enough because our bar is set too high. Set your goals with wisdom and patience in mind. If waking up early and exercising is a new habit, then choose a realistic time for your alarm and a proper expectation for your exercise as you get started.

2. Our dream or reward is not grand enough to outweigh our original discomfort, thus losing your grip of momentum to stick with it. Provide the right reward and frame of mind to counter any displeasure. Perhaps your Why isn't front and center enough. Add some incentives if needed based on your motivation style. Ask someone to be a source of accountability for you as well.

3. Our choice of action steps to get you where you want to be may not be how you are wired to keep you motivated. Instead

of adjusting and trying something different, you draw the assumption you weren't built for having morning routine habits. If running doesn't fit you well, try something else.

4. We forget how much our body will resist the new habit and underestimate our addiction to old habits. We need to remind ourselves that we aren't going to want to wake up early.

Change may not be fast, and it's not always easy; but with time and effort, almost any habit can be reshaped.

CHARLES DUHIGG

When we first laid out the chapters for this book, there wasn't a habit chapter. The more we read, researched, and stepped into our own dreams, it became SO obvious to us the power our habits hold over our lives. Especially the ones that keep us in bondage to living a mediocre lifestyle and not reaching our full potential. We knew it was so important that we added this chapter to turn on the lights and take an honest look at your closet stacked with old habits. Knowledge is power for change, and we hope gaining these insights can help motivate you to make some daily habit changes, just as it did for us.

Sewing Seeds for Growth

There have been too many dreams and goals left to vanish into thin air because we let our idle motivations and desires do the walking. By design, our dreams and goals were meant to be stationary, meaning there will be time and space in between. The dreams you have require very different actions to get you there, unless you have a springboard and plan to take one big, overly optimistic leap to your final destination. For the majority, and probably even the talented springboard vaulter, this is not the case. To reach our desired destinations, we will need to start by building a new routine. So how do we counteract our desire to reach our lofty goals with the need to establish small, sustainable habits that grow us towards our goal or dream?

What if you started thinking of your life
goals, not as big, audacious things that
you can only achieve when the time is
right or when you have better resources
or when you finally catch your big break;
but instead as tiny, daily behaviors that are
repeated until success becomes inevitable?

SETH GODIN

Taking a Closer Look

How do you cultivate a habit that will nourish and feed your dream and goals? Since habits are so powerful, wouldn't it make more sense to utilize them to build momentum towards your dream? Of course! Hopefully, you know what goal you are to pursue. Now is the time to examine your routine behaviors to determine if they will get you to your goal. This is where you might find a big clue as to why you fell short in the past. Zoom in on your current routines, or the lack of, especially the morning habits, and observe how you are setting the tone and standard for the rest of your day.

Small disciplines repeated with consistency every day lead to great achievements gained slowly over time.

JOHN MAXWELL

Let's take a look at some helpful tips and principles for growth in our daily routine. As you read through each one, imagine one or two specific habits from your day. Consider your time spent in the car, what you do for lunch, your work schedule and productivity, and your free time in the evening. You can also consider the very end of your day: going to sleep, late-night snacking, reading, or scrolling social media until you pass out.

Create Habit Plans: There's nothing you can't do if you get the habits right. Target the most important opportunities and build habits in that area.

Start Small: What is one behavior you can change today?

Make It Easy: Make a list of actions that will get you closer to your dream. What are the top three that are imperative to propelling you forward? Incorporate these into your daily routine.

Do Every Day—Consistency: Consistency can help you overcome any lack of natural talent and allow you to focus on the process instead of the end goal. It transforms average habits into excellent habits.

Stacking Your Habits: When the desired behavior becomes an automatic habit, repeat the process to build and incorporate other behaviors to enhance your routine. For example, once you've built a routine around eating a healthier lunch, what is a new habit that can flow right out of that? If you build a new routine that lowers screen time in the evening, what can you now do with that new time that you have earned for yourself?

Reward Yourself: Your reward should bring you a positive sense of self, progress, and accomplishment so that you want to do it again! Habits can be fun and ought to be rewarding.

This is your time to write out what your new day could look like if it was founded on strong and helpful habits. We are going to dive deeper into our morning routine in the next chapter, so let's focus on our day and evening for now. Take a moment to think through these questions and write in your answers.

What is one new daily habit that would impact your goals and dreams?

_____

_____

_____

What would be your reward for following through on this new habit?

_____

_____

_____

What are one or two additional habits that you could build into your day or evening?

_____

_____

_____

What are one or two habits that you know need to go? How are they negatively impacting you at this point?

_____

_____

_____

An extraordinary life is all about
daily, continuous improvements in
the areas that matter most.

ROBIN SHARMA

As you begin to reshape your daily habits, include God's plan
for your day. Leaning into your faith to change the direction of
your life is one of the most powerful assets you have for momentum
and longevity to finish the race. He is also your best cheerleader to
remind you why you are trying to push through. You now believe you
have a powerful purpose for your life, and to get there you may need
some supernatural help to build your new habits!

You are **HERE**
identifying old habits that
no longer serve you.

You are **HERE**
creating new ones.

You are **HERE**
feeling hopeful in your plan.

You are **HERE**
reaching for your dream!

OWN YOUR MORNING

Based on our research and personal experience in this process, we believe morning routine habits can be the game changer to reaching our dreams and goals. When you woke up this morning, what did you do first? Think through your morning routine and what it looks like, step by step. Is there any room for improvement or increased intentionality? Now is the time to determine how you can sow seeds for growth through your morning routine and habits. What you do first each day will set the tone and course for the rest of your daily experiences. The time you choose to wake up and your first early morning actions will inspire and lead most of your other daily habits and actions. Get started with your best foot forward!

Seize The Day

What's your reason for getting out of bed in the morning?

_____

_____

_____

You have this dream, so now what? You don't want to just hold it in your hand to fade away. It's time to carve out intentional space for your dream to grow and become a reality.

> If the 'thing' you are going after
> doesn't make you move, if it's not worth
> getting out of bed for, then you won't.
>
> CHRIS CAPEHART

You have a dream — you must have a PLAN! Dedicating time for intentional growth and movement each day allows you to become the person you want to be. Who do you want to be when you wake up each morning? How do you want to meet your day? Are you satisfied with hitting the snooze button seventeen times, rolling out of bed feeling half alive, a cloud of grogginess blanketing you, stumbling to the shower, pressed for time because you pressed the snooze button one too many times? Are these seemingly quick decisions leading you closer to your dream or widening the gap between where you are and where you want to be? Neglecting your mind, body, and soul will surely lead to neglected dreams, which undoubtedly will have a long-term negative impact on your life as a whole.

The morning routine is the rudder to your dream. It steers the course. Have you ever tried to reach a destination without a rudder? I certainly have, and let me just say it didn't go as well as expected. In my defense, up until this point, I had only rented paddleboards that apparently included all the important pieces. I had no idea traveling without a rudder was optional. Even after breaking a very intense sweat as I strapped this massive piece of fiberglass to the top of a car that was clearly not built for such things, I was still excited for my very first adventure on this new, pink, shiny board. Nothing could sway my anticipation, not even the seven-mile anxiety-induced trek. I also had no idea if I had secured this thing on properly, and there was a good chance it could catch the wind and fly away at any given moment of a perfect day on the water. I arrived, walked my board down to the launching dock, and I was off. Or at least that's how I envisioned it would go. However, evidently, the only thing off was the rudder that keeps me from spinning in circles. And that is exactly what I did, spin in circles.

Your morning routine is the rudder to your day. A clearly established morning routine will recalibrate your priorities and put the less significant ones to shame. At first, it may feel like a sacrifice. Perhaps a painful one as you slowly begin to loosen the grip of your tightly held belief that your current routine is working in your favor. The moment you have your carefully considered goal in your line of sight is the moment you will want to simplify your days so you have room to move in the direction of your dream. Free from distractions and free from any confusion that may try to steer you off course. As you begin to have more clarity and your focus sharpens, you will lose sight of all you gave up. The exchange of the sacrifice you made becomes the breakthrough that will secure a great return on your investment.

Progress comes when your tasks and activities are correlated with your goals and dreams. The activities have to matter and connect to a greater purpose.

Your Morning Routine will

➡️ Allow you to maximize your full potential for the greatest chance of success.

➡️ Bring your dream to fruition.

➡️ Advance you and bring you a step closer.

➡️ Empower you to SEIZE the day!

Mornings Matter

What science says about waking up early before you enter your world for the day:

➡️ Your brain is in a clearer and creative state of mind from sleeping.

➡️ You are more available for that time of processing.

➡️ You are taking control of where your mind is going for at least the first hour.

➡️ Increases your overall efficiency and sense of well-being.

➡️ Early risers tend to go to bed earlier, improving nighttime sleep habits and increasing energy levels.

➡️ Time for exercise accelerates a plethora of benefits for the body, mind, and spirit.

So YES, you have to wake up early. Take control of your day before the chaos of the moment has a chance to enter and steer you off course. This is a protected space. It is intentionally carved out and set aside for a very important, specific purpose. But guess what, ladies and a few gentlemen. There is one critical component we may want to discuss. Who wants to guesstimate what you may want to consider doing to ensure your eyes actually open when the rooster crows? No, it's not placing a bucket of cold water strategically above your head, ready to spill when your pinkie toe begins to tingle. Although I am fairly certain this will also get the job done. Being an early riser requires you to move up your evening routine and secure an earlier bedtime slot because it all starts the night before. After much non-belief and utter delusion, I have finally conceded to the hard-learned, self-collected data which undeniably proves what time I go to bed and the activities I engage in the night before directly affect the likelihood of my early morning success.

Good Night, Good Morning

Your morning routine begins the night before. It would be a good idea to prepare for bed and prepare for morning with the same focus and attention. A good morning starts with a good night!

Each decision has a cost attached to it. If you choose to stay up until 11 pm to watch a rerun of *Friends* for the hundred-thousandth time, what price will you pay? Think about how many times you've willingly paid that price. Was it even a fair trade? Do you want to keep letting your future pass you by for a few moments of second-lived laughs? What loss are you absorbing by scrolling late at night? Have you ever once woke up feeling better about yourself after looking at everyone else's polished life right before bedtime? And don't even get me started on what that bright light is doing to your brain. Knowingly or unknowingly, these decisions are taking a toll on your life. If you are serious about your dream, and I believe you wouldn't have made it this far if you weren't, then it's time to get serious about eliminating the habits that are no longer serving you and replacing them with life-enhancing ones.

For the best chance of success, set your intentions the night before. Here are some practical tips and challenges for nighttime habits that build good morning habits:

1. Determine what time you need to go to bed and set an alarm for 1 hour prior so you can begin winding down.

2. Lay out your workout clothes for the morning.

3. Know what your workout is going to be. Do not make yourself wing it or decide in the morning.

4. Determine what tomorrow's timeline needs to be. Map out your day.

5. Create a to-do list/brain dump.

6. Read something uplifting, positive, inspiring.

7. No screen time 1 hour before bed. Say "no" to the "glow."

> You will never change your life until you change something you do daily. The secret of your success is found in your daily routine.
>
> JOHN C. MAXWELL

These steps may sound incredibly daunting at first glance. Again, remember what we covered in the last chapter. Each of these habits have a Why, and they all have a reward. What you are giving up is nothing compared to the benefit! Practicing personal development awakens the dreamer inside of you. It creates an avenue for a more meaningful approach in every aspect of our lives, including the reach towards our dreams. Incorporating these practices consistently into your morning routine will leave you feeling more balanced physically, mentally, and spiritually. In time, these morning practices will increase your energy, motivation, and confidence levels!

Meaningful Mornings

We know that mornings matter. We have every evidence and experience to show that our morning time is TREMENDOUSLY valuable and key to achieving our goals and making our dreams come true. So, what could we do with this time? Here are some ideas and examples of how your life can be blessed and enriched by solid practices and strong morning routines. As you read through them, note how your life would be impacted by more of these opportunities. Perhaps you already practice some, that is great! Challenge yourself to pick one that you will add to your routine!

Stillness-Pray-Meditate: For most of us, our days have enough tasks and to-do lists. They can leave us feeling scattered, overwhelmed, and depleted. Beginning each new day with a stillness, prayer, or meditation practice allows us to allocate specific time to pay attention to where we are and what's going on. It starts with being aware of our bodies. That very act can be calming since our bodies have internal rhythms that help us relax and re-energize. There is a lot of research into the benefits of this habit, and there are many resources to help guide you to grow in the area.

Affirmations: These are positive statements and beliefs we make about ourselves and what we want to accomplish in life. Continual practice is proven to help you become more positive in your thought life, which ultimately affects your lifestyle habits. Write out affirmations in places where you can see them. Take time to read them out loud and dwell on them daily.

Gratitude Journal: A positive plus a positive equals more positive. The benefits of applying a practice like gratitude is compounded with interest when you combine it with the practice of journaling. Write out what you are thankful for. This is a muscle that will grow in your heart and mind as you continually build a bank full of gratitude. You may not notice in a day or week, but over time you will notice increased happiness.

Gratitude turns what we have into enough, and more. It turns denial into acceptance, chaos into order, confusion into clarity... it makes sense of our past, brings peace for today, and creates a vision for tomorrow.

MELODY BEATTIE

Visualization: This is how you close the gap between where you are today and where you want to be. Mental repetition is vital for competitors, performers, and athletes. You may only have one chance to do something today, so taking the time to mentally practice is extremely valuable. While you cannot foresee everything that is going to happen, you will be more prepared to succeed when you have visualized what is on the horizon of your day. Visualizing yourself walking out the steps to your dream on a daily basis will program your brain for better focus.

Exercise: This is likely the most understood morning routine. We all know exercise is good for us. However, making the new habit of waking up early AND exerting our energy through exercise is not the easiest practice to add to our morning. If you did get up and exercise, what would you like to accomplish? What is a small step you can take to build up this habit?

Skip the Snooze Button: Sleep science indicates when you hit the snooze button, your brain and body go into another 90-minute sleep cycle! We rarely get 90 more minutes of sleep, which means when we finally get out of bed, our body is still in sleep mode. Conquering this part of our routine opens the door for many of the other routines. It is vitally important to start our day off right!

Making Your Bed: This is a simple way to help you feel good at the beginning of the day. Start your day with an accomplishment, an easy win. Within minutes of waking up, you've already completed a valuable task. Get the ball rolling and build momentum by making your bed in the morning.

Drinking Water: There is a lot of science behind this practice as well. Make it a goal to drink approximately ½ of your body weight in ounces of water. The health and wellness benefits are great, and your body will thank you for it!

Mapping Out Your Morning Routine

We have BIG dreams. We are preparing ourselves to undertake new habits that will propel us forward. As our dreams evolve, so must we. Personal development and pursuing your dreams are adjacent relatives. You cannot mature into your dream if you do not have a plan to grow in your personal life.

On a scale of 1 - 10, how motivated are you today to push forward?

_____

How much time will you need in the morning to feel a sense of accomplishment? _____

What time will you go to bed? _____
What time will you get up? _____

What are some action steps in your nighttime or morning routine that will help you grow towards your dream and goals?

_____

_____

_____

Now let's make a specific plan and map out your morning:

Your Wake Up Time: _____

For Your First 10 Minutes, You Will: _____

For Your Next _____ Minutes, You Will: _____

The key to success is to start small. Would you try to lift 200 pounds on the first day of a new workout program? Probably not. At least not without hurting yourself. You may want to consider building your muscle memory and strengthening your core foundation first. Build the muscle memory of completing a simple routine, and then add more tasks once you build some consistency.

Track your progress. Are you gaining traction? If not, it's time to adjust and reassess. This is a continual process where there will be many check-in points. As you progress, the action steps may evolve or change. Be prepared to pivot when you start to feel stagnant.

Travel Advisory Alert! Your first morning routine habits won't be your best starting out! Developing new morning habits means you will have to get up early in your morning, and for some, you'd have a better chance pole vaulting over a football field. Sometimes we set a wake-up time we aren't quite ready to welcome yet. Keep it simple as you begin to build the habit. Be willing to experiment with different formulas until you find the one that works for you. And then practice until it becomes your new way of life.

Better Together

As previously mentioned, accountability increases the likelihood we will continue to strive towards our goals and create new habits. We all understand the potential of a follow-through when someone else is counting on us. Whether it's your boss committing you to a task with a deadline, telling your child you would be at their game, or promising to lead a group, all of these commitments require us to show up because they connect another person to our integrity and character. Oftentimes, when something is only up to us, we are more likely to drop the ball, get sidetracked, and let ourselves down. Be sure to choose someone that values you and what you are trying to accomplish, so they can encourage you often and check-up in a way that you don't get defensive. You want to feel proud of yourself for even the smallest steps you have made!

The voice of accountability would ask, "How are you doing with your commitment to your morning routine?" What response would you prefer to say? You get to decide every morning which action you will take. Ultimately, you are still the one in control. Accountability just gives your heart and dream backup and support when old habits and mindsets try to deter you.

"The American Society of Training and Development (ASTD) did a study on accountability and found that you have a 65% chance of completing a goal if you commit to someone."

Four benefits of having an accountability partner:

➡️ They help you be more responsible for yourself and follow through with your commitments.

➡️ They help you stay more engaged and motivated to stay on track.

➡️ They improve your day-to-day success to reach and sustain your new habits.

➡️ They encourage you to change a stagnant mindset to a growth mindset.

Who will you ask today to be your accountability person?

_____

_____

_____

What will you specifically share about what you want to accomplish and how they can partner with you to get there?

_____

_____

_____

When will you do a check-in with them?

_____

_____

_____

You Can Master Your Morning!

Achieving a bold, made-for-greatness dream is doable for everyone—me, you, your children, your grandmother, and probably even your dog. The distance between you and your dream is made up of many individual steps. Reaching your destination requires an accumulation of all these steps in the same direction. It is in the mundane steps where the ground starts shifting. Your morning routine provides the clearance space where the magic has room to unfold. It accelerates each step by ensuring they are succinct. Setting aside a specific time every day to commit to your dream ensures the best possible chance for success. It eliminates the excuse of "I'll do it later" because we all know, even with the best intentions, later never comes. We cannot emphasize enough how important having a powerful morning routine is. It is the golden ticket. It is the sweet spot where your dream meets your new reality.

Starting your day on an individually customized rhythm allows your actions and intentions to fall into alignment with the path of your specific dream. It produces the necessary momentum to sync up your steps with great purpose and will automatically flow into the rest of your day. You will be on high alert, ready to receive and reserve anything that resembles or appears to be the same shade of beautiful vision you are trying to create.

You are **HERE**
wanting to seize your day.

You are **HERE**
clearing the space for new energy.

You are **HERE**
waking up early.

You are **HERE**
ready to create the life you want!

FORWARD
VISION

Imay be one of the most pragmatic, practical people you may ever meet. To me, visualization was some form of magic I thought others believed in because they were two degrees short of sane. I have practiced yoga for many years. I also have a mind that never slows. It keeps going and going. Every once in a while, I can produce a string of coherent thoughts, but mostly my mind is filled with the randomness and clutter of an endless to-do list, where I need to show up next, and forty-six beginning thoughts about nothing. For anyone who's ever practiced yoga for more than one day, you will understand me when I say *savasana* is the hardest part of your practice. Savasana is kind of like the pause button on your remote control. As you lay still, flat on your back with arms and legs melting into the ground beneath, your body is afforded the time to absorb all of the twists, turns, and bends you just experienced. It encourages your body to relax with every deep breath out and feel rejuvenated with each deep breath in. It also enables you to settle into a state of self-awareness by visualizing with greater depth and clarity.

I can hold a plank for 2 minutes, headstand not a problem; but the art of relaxation, now that's a challenge even the most competitive spirit inside me will shrink from. I always showed up for the physical part of yoga practice, but when savasana and visualization were introduced, I would generally check out. And by checking out, I mean roll my eyes so far into the back of my head, it was obvious there was no way I was going to buy into this madness. I skipped this part of my practice for years. I thought it wasn't omething that applied to me. Simply wasn't my thing, and I was more than okay with that notion.

You may feel the same way. And trust me when I say, I truly understand why your head is tilted as you read this chapter. But hear me out for a second.

Visualization is probably something you're already doing but have no idea. You see, I was visualizing way before I knew it was a thing that many highly successful people practiced, but I hadn't yet connected the dots. When you find yourself dating someone, do you imagine yourself getting married, having babies, and growing happily ever after together? Yep, that's visualization. As a kid, did you visualize what you wanted to be when you grew up? Maybe a doctor, a movie star, or even an astronaut. Ever think about what type of house you see yourself growing old in? Envisioning, imagining, thinking about, conceiving are all templates you already have in your possession.

If you are sitting here thinking this is something you're not good at, or you need hours more practice to figure it out, or you are terrified to let these thoughts escape because you're not sure the world can handle them, keep in mind you have been visualizing your entire life. You are further along than you may have initially thought. Throughout this chapter, we will show you how to unlock the power and intentionality of the practice that you have already been practicing.

What is Visualization?

I can't imagine I'm the first or the only person to be apathetic or suspicious of visualization. However, research tells us that the process of visualization is powerful and effective. Our brains were created for change. The concept of neuroplasticity has been researched since the late 1800's, with more distinct findings in the 1900's. It is now a well-known fact that the brain cannot tell the difference between when we visualize an action and when we actually perform the same action.

"Neuroplasticity is the ability of the brain to adapt and change." The word neuro is related to nerve cells or neurons, and the term *plasticity* refers to the nature of our brain and nervous system. Neuroplasticity is the reason teachers and therapists use repeated practice, awareness, and intentions. These repetitions create new neural pathways for learning and change in students and clients. Repeated input in the form of sensory, physical, or mental is what stimulates neuroplasticity, such as when learning to play an instrument or learning a new language.

If you are like me, you may completely understand that practice and repetition is how you grow and improve as a student, artist, athlete, and so on—but, you may not make the immediate connection between practice on the the field or in the classroom with mental repetition and visualization. Let's keep diving into the benefits and realities of this amazing tool.

A Professional Tool

You have a desire to pursue a better version of yourself. For that pursuit to be successful, your brain will need to be stimulated on a daily basis until the pathways and habits of thought become more automatic. One of the most powerful tools we can use is visualization. In my work with trauma patients whose brains hold intense emotional images with full sensory involvement from a past event, I utilize a specific type of therapy called Accelerated Resolution Therapy (Laney Rosensweig). The neurons are stimulated, allowing reprogramming of the traumatic images through a series of repetition and eye movements. They are able to keep the facts of their memories without the intense emotions that cause physical and emotional distress. Much of this therapy is used with combat veterans and has significant research-based results.

Many speakers, professional golfers, and athletes will attest to the success in their careers to visualization. They envision the hole in one, the 3-point shot, and the TED talk way before ever stepping foot on stage. The power of visualizing their speech, playing an entire game of golf, and athletic performance are all the means of training their brains to follow where they want it to go. Visualization is definitely an underutilized, brain-altering, life-changing tool that can affirm where you want to go. It is a professional level tool that unlocks skill, confidence, and preparation on a whole new level. So why isn't everyone doing this? Maybe we have a mental block against this practice because it feels less real or productive than physical repetition. Maybe the results of this practice are not instantaneous enough. We all know visualizing a promotion doesn't necessarily come with a pay raise. But again, these mental reps are what inspire and prepare us to accomplish our goals. We encourage you to open yourself up to the practice that is designed to release the power you hold inside of you. Don't miss out!

Mental Competition

As previously mentioned, you already have been visualizing events in life that you know are going to happen. In those moments, you are simply using the more conscious part of your brain to determine how your experience could go. Each time you've imagined the future or outcome of a future opportunity, you were visualizing. And each time you visualize, you are creating a competition in your mind. Visualization requires reframing your current life to your future life, what could happen next and how you want it to go. This is where you run into the battleground of your

unconscious, old, deeply entrenched beliefs and thoughts

vs

your new level of consciousness, which includes your hopes, dreams, aspirations

As you begin to create new perspectives and beliefs for your new life, you are now "competing" with the muscle of your old unconscious programming. This was an "Aha moment" for us.

Now we get why it takes so much mental work to push through and change, and is often where we quit too soon or give up. Don't give up on yourself! If you are of a competitive nature, then you can view this as a challenge—the old against the new—and activate your desire to win to push through. Otherwise, let your desire for your dream and your faith fuel you to take charge of your brain in a conscious present-day mode.

To win the battle, your weapon will be to consistently practice over and over your new attitudes, beliefs, and behaviors to reprogram your divinely created neurons to work for you. Visualization will be your practice field, bringing all the visual, sensory, and spiritual thoughts and images to your brain to take in and to be absorbed experientially on a daily basis. This repeated process will create new connections, which over time will become your new default! At some point, you will begin to notice something very different about how you view yourself and what used to be a mere hopeless wish is now becoming your reality. If you have never hit a game winning shot, then your unconscious mind will exist in that space of "never" from the past and project "can't" or "won't" for the future. Visualizing hitting the game winning shot over and over again not only benefits your form and physical preparation, it allows a new level of consciousness to build up that prepares you to actually take that shot because you believe that you can and will make it.

> When we visualize goals as complete,
> it creates a conflict in our subconscious
> mind between what we are visualizing
> and what we currently have. Our minds
> are hard-wired to resolve such conflicts
> by working to create a current reality that
> matches the one we have envisioned.
>
> JACK CANFIELD

Your thoughts and beliefs dictate your reality. And guess what? You get to choose what you think and believe. You also have permission to reserve the right to change your mind at any given time. I beg you to please not relinquish this right. If you are clinging to a belief that you don't have enough money to start that new business venture, then that is what you will hold onto as truth. And low and behold, you will be right. The majority of us are living in the narrow space of our comfort zones and limiting beliefs. Certainty is what we crave, and our left-side brain ensures we are fed our daily dose. But when you challenge this part of your brain by applying visualization you begin creating a colorful, detailed, specific version of your future self and the left brain considers it could actually be true. When this shift takes place, your past beliefs no longer hold power to dictate your personality and behavior. Your future self rises to the occasion and begins directing your steps. You're no longer wandering in the wide-open space. You now have a detailed road map to guide you from your current state to your desired new reality.

> The only way to have a powerful 'present' is by advancing courageously toward a specific future. When you're committed to a bigger future, your present becomes far less predictable.

BENJAMIN HARDY

Designing a specific picture of who you need to be and what you are trying to achieve will generate movement and give you a deep desire to take action.

Practice Makes YOU Possible

Step 1: Know what you want. What is your dream or goal? What is your desired result? You have likely heard the phrase, "without a clear vision, the people perish." This means you will get lost in the unknowns or your own limitations. Know where you are headed and why you are headed there.

Step 2: Get specific. Where are you now? How will you get where you want to go? Detail every step you would take. What would a day in the life of your future look like? What are you wearing, how do you feel, what emotions are present, what smell is in the air? The more specific and detailed you are, the more likely your brain will begin to accept and adapt to your new level of consciousness.

Step 3: Attach emotions, positive personality traits, and affirmations. Notice how you are confident, happy, driven with purpose, excited to start your day as you envision yourself accomplishing your goals. What qualities will you need to start that new business or embark on a weight-loss journey? How will it feel when you reach your dream?

Step 4: Be on the lookout. Think about the array of activities relevant to progressing towards your dream or goal. As you open up your vision, new opportunities will present themselves. Or, more accurately, you will begin to take notice. You are providing extra space and time to study your roadmap, understand your directions, and never miss a turn.

Step 5: Take daily actions by adopting visualization into your current state. Make any necessary adjustments to invite life into your dream. Repeat every day. You will want your body and mind to be in a relaxed, calm, and focused state. For optimal results, we highly encourage you to incorporate this practice somewhere in your morning routine where your head is clear, worries haven't found their way in yet, and you are free to focus in peace.

Growing Forward

Even though there are times we feel the opposite may be true, nothing our minds do is purposeless or random. We spin in circles when we restrict ourselves with negative beliefs or don't have a clear direction. There is no better time, or actually no other time, than right here and right now to define your destination. By visualizing, you are reprogramming deep below the surface where your newly found friend, the subconscious mind, will be eager to help you do whatever it takes to secure the life you envisioned.

Here are four more tips to visualization that will enhance your practice. Do not let these pages and chapters slide by, grab hold of them. You CAN see opportunity and growth in your future. You CAN try something new and different without assuming the worst about it or yourself. You CAN take steps to shape your future and prepare your mind for all of the many victories and obstacles that are ahead of you. This is all to help build a sustainable confidence and expand your assurance about yourself:

➡ Visualize yourself as you want to be.

➡ Dream big for your future.

➡ Do one thing that scares you every day.

➡ Challenge your inner critic.

As you go forward, grow! We often struggle with the past and replay a failure or missed opportunity over and over again. Have you ever left a meeting, a dinner table, or a date and wished that you had another shot at it? We may get stuck in a loop, watching the rerun in our mind over and over again, wishing so bad that things went differently. Real, healthy visualization pushes us forward and through the past. Instead of being a captive of our past, we get to focus on the future that will be different next time. Turn yourself forward facing, forward marching. Replaying an old memory is not as beneficial as building strength and confidence for your next opportunity.

As you expand and evolve, so will your dream and so will your vision. Incorporate new elements and examine daily what you can do today to make yourself better tomorrow. Over time, with intentional practice, you will be amazed when the once impossible thought finds its way into the realm of highly possible. What you think, you most certainly can create, if you have the courage to believe.

You are **HERE**
expanding the vision for yourself.

You are **HERE**
drawing a detailed picture.

You are **HERE**
where impossible seems possible.

You are **HERE**
with the courage to believe!

STEADFAST AND PURSUE

S tay steadfast and pursue your dream. There will be times when things don't work out as planned. Keeping the dream in sight will help you see through the discomfort of failing. Failure will take on a new definition for you, as it can be a catalyst for growth towards your purpose and your dream. It will no longer hold the same value it once did. It will make you ask for more. Until you start walking towards your dream, you may not ask for very much from life.

I recently crossed paths with such a perfect analogy that, instead of trying to paraphrase and run the risk of butchering it into a million unrecognizable pieces, I will share it here in its true form:

Salmon.

Yes, I said salmon. Not only are they rich in omega-3 acids and a great source of protein, but they are also masters at teaching us about the art of staying steadfast while pursuing our dreams. God-created these remarkable creatures with the ability to seemingly defy gravity and swim up waterfalls. Just think for one second about the level of focus you would need to attempt to swim up a waterfall. Even this powerful current isn't enough to knock them off course because their eagerness to thrive and reach their destination overshadows any lack of skill, fear of failure, or unplanned detours. You see, what salmon innately know is how to turn themselves—from center to tail—into the powerful current coming at them. When they hit it squarely, the impact launches them out and further up the waterfall.

It is our leaning into our dream, leaning into our discomfort, and leaning into our growth areas again and again that propels us forward. In order to not be swept away by the undercurrents of life, we must stay faithful to the vision we have for our life and our future. We must face our daily experiences with enough grace to allow room for our perspectives to expand. The pursuit of your dream will not always look picture perfect. There is no doubt you will encounter many obstacles along the way, but to keep the dream alive, you must face these challenges head-on. It is the repeated impact that reveals our willingness, which enables us to experience the depth of our pursuit.

First, it is an intention. Then a behavior. Then a habit. Then a practice. Then a second nature. Then it is simply who you are.

BRENDON BURCHARD

Our lives are made up of these seemingly small decisions that, when looked at independently, don't appear to have a significant impact. But we are convinced every choice in the direction of your dream serves as a catalyst to move you forward. Even the slightest degree of change will alter the course and put you closer to the path you were created for. We understand that some of these small choices come with an enormous price tag. It is grueling work to face yourself and make peace with your past. Kicking your limiting beliefs to the curb requires the strength of a lumberjack who can saw through a tree stump in 30 seconds or less. Putting life-debilitating shame to rest demands perseverance and undeniable stamina. And just when you thought you made it out of the woods, the external forces working against you remind you of their dream-crushing presence.

It takes work to shed yourself of the beliefs, mindsets, and unhealthy habits keeping you from pursuing something that makes you feel alive and fulfilled. And doing that work is a choice. Just as it's a choice to stop endless scrolling, stop giving busyness permission to creep in and rob you of your precious days. And please, pretty please, stop convincing yourself the universe has to align in perfect harmony before you can begin creating a life you are excited to live. The road before us will always have obstacles and detours. Remain steadfast and pursue your dreams. You are HERE for a reason, and your dreams will IMPACT the world around you.

The Choice Is Yours

This book was designed to serve as a guide to build a framework that will support your dreams. We have relentlessly prayed for the path to be revealed. We have scoured the internet, read thousands of articles, immersed ourselves in endless resources, workshops and even watched a video on skin picking because, well… now that I think about it, I'm not actually sure how we fell down into that rabbit hole. We have willingly subjected ourselves to trial and error and failed forward enough times to fill every single page of our journals. And it was all done to uncover these tried and true practices to equip you with the necessary insight, skills, and awareness for the clearest path to success.

You are here, exactly where you are supposed to be. Inside, you, and you alone, contains all the hard-fought-for gifts, talents, wisdom, and experiences to strive towards whatever dream your heart reveals. There may be some areas you are already crushing and areas that are in desperate need of some Miracle-Gro. There will be old, no-longer-serving-you things you will need to let go of. There will be new things you will need to pick up, and there will be things that are so sacred you need to guard them with every ounce of your being.

The choice is yours, and the time is now. Your God-inspired dream has been waiting for the green light to flash. Its progress requires daily intentional choices, thoughts, and actions to provide the sustenance to elevate it into your brand-spanking-new reality. Nourish it with daily disciplines that will enhance your motivation, confidence, and courage along the way. In the midst of it all, you will learn to show lots of love, gratitude, and grace for yourself as you journey to keep growing with your dream! You now have a new level of awareness of all the pieces on how to build the life you love. It is up to you to use them to the best of your ability.

Your dreams are the pathway to influence others with hope for their future. This is where legacy begins. You Are Here. Perhaps you have never thought you had anything to offer anyone, including yourself. Perhaps you have always known but just couldn't find your way.

Your Legacy

Legacy, like your dream, is embedded deep in your heart. Search for it, begin to cultivate what's in your heart to do, and you will see your passion grow outward towards significance. Once you ignite that passion and keep fanning the fire, it will spread, ushering in new energy and a new outlook on your life. This is the precursor to the bigger picture now coming into view. Legacy is not about money or possessions. It is what you put out beyond yourself that goes into the world. You were called to greatness, and this is the part where you will begin to sow seeds of significance and meaning based on who you have become and your heart's desire to share it!!

About two years ago, the word "legacy" began to surface in my spirit and in my heart. Whenever that happens, I start searching to discover what God is saying to me. In secular terms, the word legacy is primarily about what someone has left us in terms of money or possessions. In a much grander, divine way, it's about who we are, what we did, how we treated others, how we inspired others, how we encouraged others to do the same. It is a part of your living here on earth that goes beyond who you are long after you are gone. I asked myself, what do I want to be remembered for? How can I leave an impression on my family, grandkids, clients, co-workers, and friends for their own lives? How can my legacy become an eternal gift for them to pursue and create for their own lives? How can your life be a gift to those around you to inspire them on their journey?

Leading a legacy life has become a motivational source that fuels my personal and spiritual development for today and for God's greater plan for me in the future. All of that is definitely not going to grow without an intentional plan each day to get me there. The reason I know this is because when I didn't have an intentional daily routine, I just wasn't able to extend to the "more" part of my life I was seeking. Once I started to cultivate and personalize my mornings with God and to take control of my thought life and actions, things definitely started to change. Even today, I am still implementing steps that will launch me forward towards leaving an impactful legacy. You see, leaving a legacy of impact on others is one of my dreams. Our dreams are not only for us to benefit from. There is a much bigger purpose: for us to fulfill our dream and impact the world around us. We are all entitled to a beautifully rich legacy.

That dream in your heart is not a frilly distraction, a ridiculous idea, a muted hope. It is a solid purpose; it is a righteous plan; it is a trumpet.

BRENDON BURCHARD

Your dream will help you fill in the gaps. In the pursuit, you develop the stories that others will tell. Fulfilling your purpose allows you to collect and compile your story. Through these stories, you'll leave behind an impact to enrich the lives of others. So, the dreams you think no one cares about, go get them! Fill in the mundane spaces of life with a meaningful pursuit of things that make you feel alive, and watch your legacy unfold.

God calls all people to pursue their unique gifts, to discover the ways He wants to influence the world through them, to leave a trail of beauty.

EMILY FREEMAN

Legacy is born out of your desire to follow your dream. It creates an energy and a desire to live beyond yourself, to flow out for impact. It's about believing you have something important and valuable to share with others. Your legacy will help you stay committed and steadfast throughout your journey. Your legacy will inspire you to pursue your biggest goals and reach for your dreams. Meditate on that for a moment.

Be brave and write down what you want your legacy to be to the world and date it.

_____

_____

_____

Picture This

Visualize yourself committed to intentional daily choices to touch your dream. See yourself getting up in the morning following through with all the small steps that will gradually achieve your goal! See yourself feeling more confident and good about yourself than ever! See yourself being open to growth and more opportunities than you ever thought you would say yes to. Notice your excitement. Notice that you get up in the morning feeling different; notice how you are already sharing your new energy with others and how they want to be around you. You are already influencing them, and now you realize you want to do so much more. YOU ARE HERE believing you were made for more and have a legacy to share with others. See yourself setting new goals and how happy and joyful you feel doing it. See yourself with those you will impact and how that feels compatible with your core being.

Committing to goals, dreams, and legacy will determine how you show up every day. It will influence your day-to-day decisions and choices. Visualize your new self showing up and inspiring others to believe that their life has meaning too. They can also begin the journey you started. See yourself feeling important in a humble way, knowing deep in your heart you are making a difference.

Our hope for you is that somewhere in the midst of what we have shared, something has inspired you to dare to dream again, to think BIG, and take that first small step towards it. Now it's all up to you.

What's your next decision or choice going to be? Lock in on that first step, pursue it and be steadfast to complete it. Celebrate it and then keep building; we know you can do it!

You are **HERE**
leaning into your future self.

You are **HERE**
embarking on your dream.

You are **HERE**
defining your legacy.

YOU ARE **HERE**!

citation notes

Introduction

- Dooley, J. L. (2019). *Own your everyday: Overcome the pressure to prove and show up for what you were made to do.* WaterBrook.

Chapter 1

- Warren, R. (2007). *The purpose Driven life: What on earth am I here for,* Rick Warren. Zondervan.

- Dweck, Carol S. (2016). *Mindset.* Ballantine Books

- Didion, Joan. (1979) *The White Album.* Simon & Schuster.

- 465. George Bernard Shaw (1856-1950). Respectfully Quoted: A Dictionary of Quotations. 1989. (n.d.). https://www.bartleby. com/73/465.html.

- Bennett, R. F. (n.d.). *Favorite authors.* BrainyQuote. https://www. brainyquote.com/quotes/.

Chapter 2

- Sisgold, S. (n.d.). *Limited beliefs.* Psychology Today. https://www. psychologytoday.com/us/blog/life-in-body/201306/limited-beliefs.

- Blackman, A. (2021, May 20). *What are self-limiting beliefs? +how to overcome them successfully.* Business Envato Tuts+. https://business. tutsplus.com/tutorials/what-are-self-limiting-beliefs--cms-31607.

- Kivoski, Robert T. (2020, July 30). *"It's not what you say out of your mouth that determines your life, it's what you whisper to yourself that has the most power."* PositLive. https://positlive.com/its-not-what-you-say-out-of-your-mouth-that-determines-your-life-its-what-you-whisper-to-yourself-that-has-the-most-power/.
- Tracy, B. (2019, January 21). *15 quotes to overcome YOUR SELF-LIMITING BELIEFS. SUCCESS.* https://www.success.com/15-quotes-to-overcome-your-self-limiting-beliefs/.
- Huber, C. (n.d.). Cheri HUBER: *Living Spiritual Teachers: Quotes: Spirituality & practice.* Cheri Huber | Living Spiritual Teachers | Quotes. https://www.spiritualityandpractice.com/explorations/teachers/cheri-huber/quotes.
- Hibbert, D. C. (2014, July 12). *Self-Esteem vs. Self-worth: Q & A W/ Dr. CHRISTINA Hibbert*: Dr. Christina Hibbert. Dr. Christina Hibbert | Dr. Christina Hibbert.com. https://www.drchristinahibbert.com/self-esteem-vs-self-worth/.
- Robbins, Tony. https://www.facebook.com/photo?fbid=387860869369932&set=a.355143759308310
- Brown, Brené. https://www.quotemaster.org/qb5912864a846281568ead912fc6965bb

Chapter 3

- Hayden, G. (n.d.). braintrainingtools.org. http://www.braintrainingtools.org/skills/followingthrough-is-the-only-thing-that-separates-dreamers-from-people-that/.
- Ezra 10:4 (NIV)

- Merriam-Webster. (n.d.). *Busyness*. Merriam-Webster. https://www.merriam-webster.com/dictionary/busyness.

- Brown Brené. (2015). *Daring greatly: How the courage to be Vulnerable transforms the way we live, Love, parent, and lead.* Penguin Books Ltd.

Chapter 4

- 2 Corinthians 5:17 (NLT)
- Psalm 139:13-14 (NIV)
- Philippians 4:8 (NIV)
- Rock, D. (n.d.). *New study shows humans are on autopilot nearly half the time*. Psychology Today. https://www.psychologytoday.com/us/blog/your-brain-work/201011/new-study-shows-humans-are-autopilot-nearly-half-the-time.
- Winch, G., About the author Guy Winch is a licensed psychologist who is a leading advocate for integrating the science of emotional health into our daily lives. His three TED Talks have been viewed over 20 million times, & Samper, J. (2017, January 10). *5 ways to build lasting self-esteem*. ideas.ted.com. https://ideas.ted.com/5-ways-to-build-lasting-self-esteem/.
- Maxwell, J. C. (2011). *Put your dream to the Test: 10 questions to help you see it and seize it.* Thomas Nelson, Inc.
- Merton, Thomas. https://www.goodreads.com/quotes/243053-you-do-not-need-to-know-precisely-what-is-happening

Chapter 5

- Bissett, Josie. https://www.quotetab.com/quote/by-josie-bissett/dreams-come-a-size-too-big-so-we-can-grow-into-them
- Xplore. (n.d.). Woodrow Wilson Quotes. BrainyQuote. https://www.brainyquote.com/quotes/woodrow_wilson_121798.
- Levoy, G. (n.d.). *Dreams don't come true, they are true.* Psychology Today. https://www.psychologytoday.com/us/blog/passion/201604/dreams-dont-come-true-they-are-true.
- Maxwell, J. C. (2019, December 19). *What is your dream?* SUCCESS. https://www.success.com/what-is-your-dream/.
- Shelton, Trent. (2019). *The Greatest You.* Nelson Books.

Chapter 6

- Merriam-Webster. (n.d.). *Why.* Merriam-Webster. https://www.merriam-webster.com/dictionary/why.
- Goodreads. (n.d.). *A quote by Mark Twain.* Goodreads. https://www.goodreads.com/quotes/505050-the-two-most-important-days-in-your-life-are-the.
- Goleman, D. (1998). *Working with emotional intelligence.* Bantam Books.
- Proverbs 16:26 (TPT)
- Robbins, Mel. (2019, Feb 28). https://www.youtube.com/watch?v=cO2x14aPq8M

Chapter 7

- Einstein, A. (n.d.). *The mind that opens to a new idea never returns to ITS... at QuoteTab.* QuoteTab. https://www.quotetab.com/ quote/by-albert-einstein/the-mind-that-opens-to-a-new-idea-never-returns-to-its-original-size.
- Nietzsche, Friedrich. Xplore. (n.d.). *Friedrich Nietzsche Quotes.* BrainyQuote. https://www.brainyquote.com/quotes/friedrich_ nietzsche_103819.
- Hauge, O. H., Bly, R., & Hedin, R. (2008). *The Dream We Carry: Selected and last poems of Olav H. Hauge.* Copper Canyon Press.
- Esposito, E., 2015. The Essential Guide to Writing S.M.A.R.T. Goals. [Blog] Smartsheet, Available at: <https://www. smartsheet.com/blog/essential-guide-writing-smart-goals> [Accessed 9 February 2018].

Chapter 8

- Claire, K. K. S. (2014). *The confidence code: The science of getting more.* HarperCollins.
- Wikimedia Foundation. (2021, July 19). *Confidence.* Wikipedia. https://en.wikipedia.org/wiki/Confidence.
- Biles, Simone. https://girlsleadership.org/blog/can-simone-biles-confidence-be-taught/

Chapter 9

- Elrod, H. (2018). *The miracle morning: The not-so-obvious Secret guaranteed to transform your life before 8am.* Hal Elrod International, Inc.
- Duhigg, C. (2014). *The power of habit: Why we do what we do in life and business.* Random House Trade Paperbacks.
- ScienceDaily. (2014, August 8). *How we form habits, change existing ones.* ScienceDaily. https://www.sciencedaily.com/releases/2014/08/140808111931.htm.
- Clear, James. https://jamesclear.com/why-is-it-so-hard-to-form-good-habits
- Company, T. J. M. (2013, May 6). *What's so critical about simple, daily practices?* John Maxwell. https://www.johnmaxwell.com/blog/whats-so-critical-about-simple-daily-practices/.
- Ezenwa, F. H. (2021, January 26). *Purpose archives.* Allround Achievers. https://allroundachievers.com/tag/purpose/.

Chapter 10

- Capehart, Chris. (2015). *Step.* Published in the United States of America, 2015.
- Elrod, H. (2018). *The miracle morning: The not-so-obvious Secret guaranteed to transform your life before 8am.* Hal Elrod International, Inc.

- John C. *Maxwell quote: You'll never change. Quote of Quotes.* (2019, May 19). https://quoteofquotes.com/john-c-maxwell-quote-never-change-your-life-something-you-daily-secret-success-daily-routine/.
- Beattie, M. (n.d.). *Melody Beattie Quotes (author of CODEPENDENT no more).* Goodreads. https://www.goodreads.com/author/quotes/4482.Melody_Beattie.
- Hanke, S. (2018, August 14). *Council post: Three steps to overcoming resistance.* Forbes. https://www.forbes.com/sites/forbescoachescouncil/2018/08/14/three-steps-to-overcoming-resistance/?sh=1b0b721e5eae.

Chapter 11

- Wikimedia Foundation. (2021, July 26). *Neuroplasticity.* Wikipedia. https://en.wikipedia.org/wiki/Neuroplasticity.
- Rosensweig, L. (2021, April 25). *Treating trauma.* Accelerated Resolution Therapy. https://acceleratedresolutiontherapy.com/.
- Canfield, J. (2019, December 2). *Visualization techniques to manifest desired outcomes. Jack Canfield.* https://www.jackcanfield.com/blog/visualize-and-affirm-your-desired-outcomes-a-step-by-step-guide/.
- Dweck, C. (2021, February 5). Carol Dweck: *A summary of the two mindsets.* Farnam Street. https://fs.blog/2015/03/carol-dweck-mindset/.

- Hardy, B. (2020, April 30). *Ready to commit 100% to your Dreams? Here are the 10 steps*. Benjamin P. Hardy. https://benjaminhardy. com/ready-to-commit-100-to-your-dreams-here-are-the-10-steps/.

Chapter 12

- NEPO, M. A. R. K. (2020). *Book of awakening: Having the life you want by being present to the life you have*. RED WHEEL WEISER.
- Burchard, B. (2017). *High performance habits: How extraordinary people become that way*. Hay House, Inc.
- *The blog*. Emily P. Freeman. (n.d.). https://emilypfreeman.com/ blog/page/111/?TB_iframe=true&width=921.6&height=921.6.

acknowledgments

Carol Burmood

To my loving God. Without that night of divine appointment and my yes to you for life, I wouldn't be writing this. When you found me, my life was a mess without a direction in sight. It took quite a few years to dig through the layers to heal all the broken places. You placed me in spiritual homes that nourished me until I began to get a new hunger for growth, not just for myself anymore, but for others. Slowly I began to see myself through your eyes, and potential dreams started to come into view. The message of this book is one of those dreams, and I am forever grateful for your patience with me all those years; you never gave up… and by your grace, I didn't either.

To my husband Dean. There is no way that without your unquestionable love and positive support that I would be where I am today. When I wanted to go back to college and to workshops galore, you said yes. You even went to marriage retreats, church seminars, and seminary classes along the way. And in the last year, you gave up weekends, mornings, and nights for the writing of this project. You made room for me to follow my heart to be more in order to do great things in this world for others. You have always been a source of God's peace for my heart and how we live our lives every day. For all that and so much more, know you are loved and valued.

To my daughter Ali. Your life gave my life purpose when I didn't have any. God brought you into my world fully knowing you would become a driving force for me to become a stronger, wiser woman to prepare you for life ahead. I have watched you work through many hills and valleys of your own, only to rise to the top and then stretch for even more. You have truly inspired me to believe in myself more and go for it. Anyone that comes within your reach will be challenged to change as you are a mega releaser of hope, confidence, and empowerment… gifted to move mountains. Super proud XOXO.

To my Pastor, Kurt Parker. Thank you for inviting me to partner with you and Harborside Church to bring healing and wholeness to others. Your passion for people finding God and their purpose is evident in all you do!

To Tom Goodlet, Pastor, Publisher, Author, Life Coach, Speaker, and Friend. A few years ago, we had our first conversation about your writing, and it opened the door in my mind that just maybe, that quiet dream of writing a book could possibly come to life for me. Thank you for that first talk (and all the other ones too). Without all of your yeses to God's leading for your life I wouldn't have had my chance to say yes to collaborating with you on my first project of pen to paper. Not long after, God literally placed Two Penny Publishing in your hands and brought my dream to reality.

To Desiree, Co-Author, Friend, Trailblazer. When we met over 10 years ago, we had no clue that we would be penning a book together. There were many no's to teaming up along the way until finally, you said yes to teaching with me. I am so glad that you did because honestly I don't think I had the courage to tackle all of my dreams on my own at first. Thank you for all your yes's, especially this one, to write You Are Here. You are the best writing partner anyone could ever have. You have the strength of a superhero… Commitment until completion (no matter what), focus, strong work ethic (with coffee can push through for days), love for God and his people, funny, passionate (really passionate) about people building a life they love and having the vision for how to get there, and a beautiful writer just to name a few.

To all of my courageous clients who allowed me the privilege of stepping into the inner workings of your life to help you find your way through to your destination of greatness. Your transparency taught me so much, and I have been honored to know you. Keep reaching, don't ever quit, and trust God to help you build a life you love.

The counseling process is about making a healthy choice to become a better version of yourself, and sometimes we just need a little help getting there. Once you know your true identity, you are on your way!

To my grandchildren, Ethan, Ella, and Emme, may you always believe that you can do whatever dreams God has put in your heart to fulfill. Be brave and believe! Let's write a book! XOXO

Desiree Collis

First and foremost, I want to thank God for the unconditional love and unrelenting grace that has been poured into my life. I thank Him for the second, and third, and fourth, and fifth chances that I have been given. I hope to live my life in a way that earns the blessings I have been afforded.

A big shout out to my fearless, awe-inspiring, ever humble, dream-chasing co-author Carol Burmood for believing in me long before I ever knew to believe in myself. For all the books she "loaned" me to never be returned, that expanded my perspective and stretched me beyond what I knew was possible. And for that mustard seed of faith she gave me a long time ago. She has richly poured into my life encouragement, hope, and has been one of the main mentors who has shaped me into the person I am today. I will be forever grateful for the wisdom she has imparted and for taking me under her wing to help strengthen my own identity. I promise to give every next opened door my all.

This book would not be possible had our paths not crossed over ten years ago. Little did either of us know what a beautiful friendship would blossom from that encounter. It is such a privilege and honor to learn and grow from one of the most beautiful, authentic, deeply caring women the world has to offer. Her heart and passion for people is truly something to admire. I can still remember the day she asked me to be her co-author to what will be our very first of many books. I was unsure of my YES at the time. I was also unsure why she was so inclined to place so much trust in me. But today I know why.

Thank you for your continuous support, soft pushes, reeling me in when I drifted off course, insightfully deep conversations, patience to let me get to the end of myself when my OCD would kick in, and for showing up as long as it took to bring this book to completion.

I also want to thank my mom, who instilled in me a strong spirit.

She was a force to be reckoned with. Although she is deeply missed, it was through her passing that I was given new life. A new abundant life with a new perspective, a new purpose, and new meaning that I may not have found any other way. I believe this was a gift my mom left for me and the reason this book exists.

Thank you to my dad, who deeply rooted in me a strong work ethic and determined nature that has served me well. "Where there's a will, there's a way" was ingrained in me from a very young age. At times the book writing process can be grueling, and this is where I found the strength to get back up, push harder, drink more caffeine, and get the job done.

I want to thank my dear friends Kent and Jane for one of the most important long-term friendships that I will forever hold on to and cherish. Kent, you are truly one of a kind. You are one of the most amazing mentors a girl could ever ask for. Jane, you are one of the most authentic, caring, giving souls around these parts of town. Words cannot express the imprint you have left on my life. Your constant support, encouragement, and love for my family has not gone unnoticed. I'm grateful you have allowed me to be an extension of your family. I have reached for more because I wanted to be the person you already thought I was.

Lastly, I want to thank my kids, Tristan, Kayleigh, Justin, and my semi-surrogate son Andrew for the many, and I mean many challenges that have molded me into being a better parent and leader. I am stronger and wiser because of all of you and hope to show up every day to give you the level of love, inspiration, and support each one of you deserves. One of my intentions for writing this book was to let it serve as a testimony that dreams are possible. I pray each one of you discovers what lights your soul on fire and begins walking towards it with an open heart, unrelenting courage, and undeniable belief that it is possible for you too!

about the authors

Carol Burmood is a Licensed Mental Health Counselor with LifeImpact Counseling. She is super passionate about helping people discover and bring purpose-to-dreams-to-real life. With over 20 years of experience, she has a unique style of combining faith and "living with intentional strategies" to achieve your purpose-driven goals and dreams. She believes everyone is hard-wired to become and live the best version of their lives possible and, in turn, to help others. Carol co-authored MentorUS, a book designed to walk couples through premarital counseling for her church and community, and has led various personal growth groups and mentoring.

Carol lives in Florida with her husband, Dean of 23 years and daughter, son-in-law, and three amazing grandchildren.

Desiree Collis is a mother, Certified Life Coach, Certified Yoga Instructor, and unceasing seeker of knowledge. She graduated magna cum laude from the University of South Florida with a degree in Social Work and has always had a heart for helping people strive to find their full potential. She is on a mission to share her hard-earned knowledge in a practical and relevant way to impact those who seek to transform their mind, body & spirit. Desiree's heart for people is to help them discover and visualize how to move forward from where they are in their current life and step into the future utilizing all of their gifts, talents, and full potential. She currently resides in Florida with her three children.

For more go to Lifeimpactcoaching.us

Made in the USA
Columbia, SC
31 August 2021

44136073R00150